CHUCK COLSON

Books in the **Today's Heroes** Series

Ben Carson

Chuck Colson

Andre Dawson

Dave Dravecky

Billy Graham

Dave Johnson

Joni's Story

Colin Powell

Becky Tirabassi

CHUCK COLSON

by W. Terry Whalin

ZondervanPublishingHouse

Grand Rapids, Michigan

A Division of HarperCollinsPublishers

Chuck Colson
Copyright 1994 by W. Terry Whalin

Requests for information should be addressed to:

Zondervan Publishing House
Grand Rapids, Michigan 49530

Library of Congress Cataloging-in-Publication Data

Whalin, Terry.
    Chuck Colson : from the White House to prison—how did
this ex-con become one of the most influential Christians in
the world? / by W. Terry Whalin.
        p. cm. — (Today's heroes)
    ISBN 0-310-41261-7 (softcover)
    1. Colson, Charles W.—Juvenile literature. 2. Baptists—
United States—Biography—Juvenile literature. 3. Baptist
converts—United States—Biography—Juvenile literature. 4.
Prison Fellowship—Juvenile literature. [1. Colson, Charles W.
2. Baptist converts. 3. Prison Fellowship.] I. Title. II. Series
BX6495.C5687W43 1994
286\.1\092—dc20   94-23341
[B]   CIP

                                                              AC

Edited by David Lambert
Cover design by Mark Veldheer
Cover and interior illustrations by Patrick Kelley

Printed in the United States of America

94 95 96 97 98 99/ ❖ LP /10 9 8 7 6 5 4 3 2 1

Contents

Chronology of Events

October 16, 1931. Charles Wendell Colson is born in Boston, Massachusetts.

1941. Chuck Colson begins to attend Browne and Nichols, a Cambridge preparatory school.

1949. Colson joins the Naval ROTC at Brown University and receives a full four-year scholarship.

1953. Colson graduates with distinction from Brown University, marries Nancy Billings, and is commissioned as a Second Lieutenant, United States Marine Corps.

1955. Colson leaves the Marines and becomes assistant to the assistant secretary of the Navy.

1956. Colson joins the staff of U.S. Senator Leverett Saltonstall, a Republican from Massachusetts.

1958. Colson becomes the youngest administrative assistant on Capital Hill, still working for Senator Saltonstall. He also passes the bar exam in Virginia and becomes a lawyer.

1959. Colson receives his J.D. with honors from George Washington University.

1963. Colson's first marriage ends in divorce.

1964. Colson marries Patricia Ann Hughes.

1969. Colson is appointed special counsel to President Nixon.

1971. Following President Nixon's orders, Colson "does everything possible" to stop leaks of information. He gives the press damaging information about Daniel Ellsberg.

1973. Colson leaves the White House staff to begin a law practice in Washington, D.C.

August 12, 1973. Colson accepts Jesus Christ as his Savior and is "born again."

1974. Charged with conspiracy, Colson pleads guilty to obstruction of justice. He is sentenced to one-to-three years. On June 8, he enters Fort Holabird Prison in Maryland.

1975. Colson is released from prison on January 31, after serving seven months of his sentence.

1976. Colson launches Prison Fellowship, an evangelistic ministry dedicated to taking the message of Jesus Christ to the prison inmates.

1979. Prison Fellowship International founded.

1991. Prison Fellowship has expanded to forty-eight states and forty countries.

1993. Colson is awarded the Templeton Prize for Progress in Religion—worth over one million U.S. dollars. He donates the entire amount to Prison Fellowship.

1994. Chuck Colson continues as the founder and chairman of the board of Prison Fellowship International. The ministry has a staff of two hundred-eighty and coordinates nearly fifty thousand volunteers in the U.S. and thousands more in fifty-four other nations. The ministry works in nearly eight hundred prisons and institutions in the U.S.

1

Always Tell the Truth

Fluffy white clouds drifted across the blue sky over Winthrop, Massachusetts. Two-story frame houses lined the street in this small community across the harbor from Boston—in fact, you could see the Boston city skyline rising in the distance. It was a quiet day; people settled in for another lazy afternoon.

CRASH! The sound of broken glass echoed through the neighborhood. A small boy with a crew cut and dark hair darted across the street, looking both ways—not for cars but rather, to see whether anyone had seen him toss that rock through a neighbor's second-story window. No one in sight. So five-year-old Chuck Colson scooted into his own backyard and quickly found some way to look busy.

Did anyone see me? Chuck wondered. He'd catch it if anyone found out about that broken glass.

Later that afternoon, Chuck heard a knock at the Colson's front door. He crept just close enough to hear but not close enough to be seen.?"

"Hello, Mr. Colson, glad you're home," a man's voice began. "This morning this rock came through my upstairs window. Do you know anything about it? I thought maybe your son Chuck—"

"Wait a minute," Chuck's dad said. "I'm sure it wasn't Chuck. If he had broken it, he'd have told me." Mr. Colson called back into the house, "Chuck! Come here! Did you break Mr. Walfred's window?"

Head down, eyes focused on the ground, Chuck Colson shuffled toward his father and his neighbor. The five-year-old battled inside: *What should I say? If I tell the truth, I'll be in big trouble. But if I lie—"*

"Chuck, I asked you a question," Mr. Colson said. "Did you break that window?"

"Yes, Father," Chuck said slowly. "I broke it."

The lessons of truth had been taught well and often in the Colson home. And no matter how badly Chuck wanted to avoid punishment, he couldn't lie to his father.

On another afternoon, a year later, the wind blew gently through the green trees on Chuck's street. Six now, Chuck played with a small airplane glider with a rubber-band propeller. *How far will this airplane go?* Chuck wondered. *All the way to my neighbor's yard?* He tested it. *Maybe it would fly better if it had some extra weight to it,* he thought. *Like a firecracker.*

With string, Chuck tied a small firecracker to the plane. Then he twirled the rubber-band propeller, touched a match to the fuse of the firecracker, and quickly let the plane go. It sailed across Chuck's neighbor's yard.

Below the plane, completely unaware of what was happening above his head, Chuck's neighbor sat shelling peas.

BAM! The glider exploded in mid-air, and the bowl of peas went sailing across the yard, scattering peas everywhere. Doors and windows from the houses in the neighborhood flew open. Chuck's parents ran into the backyard. "Chuck," they said, sniffing the smell from the exploding firecracker, "what was that explosion? Did *you* have anything to do with it?"

Once again, even though he knew it might get him in trouble, Chuck had to tell his father the truth. "Yes."

"Well, you go see Mr. Banister right now and apologize," his dad said.

Chuck turned away. "And Chuck?"

"Yes, Dad?"

"Help him pick up his peas."

Chuck grinned as he walked away. How he loved to pull a good practical joke! And what an expression on Mr. Banister's face!

But Chuck was learning more in those years than how to be a practical joker. Although he didn't realize it at the time, he was learning some far more valuable lessons that would serve him well in the future: to tell the truth and to apologize for his mistakes.

*   *   *

Winthrop, Massachusetts, was going through many changes during those years of Chuck Colson's childhood. And most of the changes weren't good. Many people had no jobs. People stood in long lines called breadlines, waiting for free food. Many of the Colsons' friends and neighbors were standing in those lines because they had no money for food.

Thankful to have a steady job during such difficult times, Chuck's father was a bookkeeper in a meat-packing plant. But he worked over fifty hours a week—including Saturdays. Besides the long hours, he didn't see much hope for improving his family's financial condition if he kept at that job. So Wendell Colson decided to become a lawyer. He began to attend law school at night.

Going to college was a bold step for Chuck's dad. No one on either side of Chuck's family had ever graduated from college. With the long days at the meat-packing plant and the nights of law school, Chuck's dad spent most of what little time he had at home studying law books. Sunday afternoon was about the only time Chuck could count on spending with his dad. On Sunday afternoons, the two of them would sit on the back steps of their frame house and talk. Chuck's dad sat on the top wooden step near the back door, and Chuck sat below him.

Those talks on the back porch steps made a lifelong impression on Chuck. But not all of that time was spent talking, because Chuck's dad spent most of his time reading and thinking about law for his classes. One afternoon, Mr. Colson carried out one of his textbooks from school, *The Art of Cross-Examination* by Francis Wellman. Chuck's dad was learning from this book how lawyers could asked pointed questions to expose lies and show the truth.

The book contained the records of many trials told word-for-word, and to Chuck they seemed like small dramas. His dad would read the book aloud, using two different voices, one deep and one high, to read the parts of the lawyer and the witness. In one trial, the lawyer, Mr. Choate, rose from his chair to cross-examine the witness, Mr. Sage.

"Where do you reside, Mr. Sage?' Chuck's dad would read in his low voice.

"At 506 Fifth Avenue," he would answer himself in the high voice.

"And what is your age now?"

"Seventy-seven years."

Whenever Mr. Colson read aloud, Chuck asked plenty of questions: "What does that mean?" "Why would they do that?"

"You see, Chuck," his father would explain, "you can't hide the truth. But people try. In a trial, lawyers are searching for the truth. And if they ask the right questions, they can get the right answers—the truth."

Other times, Mr. Colson would stare off into space and tell his son about some of the great courtroom trials—for instance, the famous "Monkey" trial in which two lawyers, Clarence Darrow and William Jennings Bryan, argued the theory of evolution. As Chuck listened, fascinated, Mr. Colson would describe the details of these cases, and what the lawyers said, and who won. And Chuck began to develop a deep love and respect for the law.

Sometimes those Sunday afternoon conversations with his dad took a different turn— they talked about excellence. Chuck's dad would say, "Whatever you put your mind to, you can do. And whatever you do in life—it doesn't matter if it's cleaning toilets—do it well. Do it with excellence. That's part of the dream of living in America. If you work hard, if you put your mind to it, you can succeed, you can get to the top."

For Chuck, "getting to the top" meant going to college full-time. He was aware, as he watched his dad struggling to work full-time and go to college at night, that no one in his family had ever gone full-time to college. *I'll be the first,* Chuck thought. *I'll go to college right out of high school.*

On another Sunday afternoon, Chuck learned something else from his father: "Some people want to get by with as little work as possible. Truth is, there are no shortcuts. No matter how small the job—do it well."

And on a different Sunday afternoon: "There is nothing more important than telling the truth. Always tell the truth—lies will destroy you."

*   *   *

While Chuck was still in grade school, his father finished law school. One afternoon, Chuck sat in a crowded auditorium to attend his dad's graduation. Soon his father would be a lawyer. Chuck's dad stood tall in his black cap and gown, walked across the stage, and accepted his law diploma. He was thirty-nine years old—far older than most of his classmates.

Soon after graduation, Chuck's dad took a job at General Foods as a lawyer. Even though he was a good lawyer, he couldn't seem to earn money as fast as Chuck's mother, Inez Colson, could spend it. Her friends called her "Dizzy," and she loved to buy the finest food and clothes and furniture. The Colson family lived on the edge of financial ruin.

One day Chuck walked home from school, his booksack thrown over his shoulder. As he turned the corner, he could see some strange men carrying furniture out his front door. Chuck instantly recognized the stuffed chair—it came from his living room.

He ran up to his house, shouting, "Hey, what are you doing with that chair?"

One of the men shrugged at Chuck. "Ask your mother, kid. We just bought it."

Inside, Chuck found his mother standing in a near-empty living room. "We've got to pay the rent somehow, Chuck." Mrs. Colson said as she tucked the money into an apron pocket.

It wasn't the only time Chuck's mom got the money to pay the rent by selling furniture and other household items. Even so, she continued to set a high standard of living for her family. One day, when Chuck was in fifth grade, she decided that Chuck wasn't getting a good education through the public schools. "You deserve the best, Chuck, and you're going to get it," she said.

That same day, she informed the public school that Chuck would no longer be attending there. Even though she'd only spent eight years in school herself, she knew that school would provide the future for her son. So Mrs. Colson marched Chuck down to one of the top private schools in the area—Browne and Nichols, in the nearby city of Cambridge. Some of Chuck's teachers were among the most brilliant minds in that part of the United States.

Always Tell the Truth   17

*   *   *

A few years later, Chuck earned a full scholarship to Brown University, making good on the promise he'd made to himself, on that long-past Sunday afternoon, to attend college. Most of his days at Brown were spent in a combination of studying, talking in all-night sessions, and going to fraternity parties. Chuck still loved firecrackers—even in his college years—but now his jokes were more complicated and took greater planning.

At two in the morning, for instance, Jack, one of Chuck's fraternity brothers, would answer the phone and hear, "Hello, this is Officer O'Conner at the 46th precinct. We've got one of your fraternity brothers down here at the station." It would be Chuck on the phone, disguising his voice by talking deep and holding a handkerchief across the mouthpiece. He would call from a phone booth across the street from his fraternity house, watching the dark windows. "We've got a Charles Colson in our jail here. It looks like he'll have to spend the night in a cell unless you can pay his three hundred dollar fine."

"Three hundred dollars!" Jack gasped. "That's a lot of money!"

"Well, if you haven't got it," Chuck growled, stifling his laughter, "we'll just throw him in jail. Doesn't matter to me."

"No, no," Jack insisted, rapidly waking up. "We'll see if we can get it together."

"Well, hurry up!" the "officer" barked into the phone, "or we'll have to lock him up. I'll give you thirty minutes." *Click.*

As Chuck watched from across the street, the lights went on throughout the fraternity house. Jack went door to door, trying to collect the three hundred dollars to keep Chuck out of jail. Ever the practical joker, Colson enjoyed every minute of watching the guys in his fraternity house work and sweat to scrape together the money. Then, when they were almost ready to make the trip to the police station to rescue him, Chuck sauntered across the street, his hands in his pockets, and let them know he was fine.

Besides the all-night talk-and-study sessions, Chuck earned a reputation at Brown University for caring about some unexpected people. In the basement of Fontz Hall, for instance, there was a barber named Larry. Several times a week, Chuck would stop by— not for a haircut but for some conversation: "How's the family, Larry? What have your kids been up to?" Chuck Colson was remembered not only as a hard worker and a practical joker but also as someone who was interested in others and who genuinely cared about them.

*   *   *

The Korean War was raging while Chuck was at school. Many of Chuck's fraternity brothers and other friends were signing up and shipping out for overseas. During Chuck's second year of college, one of his fraternity brothers, Bill Maloney, was a senior. After graduating, Bill took a commission in the Marines. When Bill would come back to Brown to visit, he would talk with great pride and enthusiasm about the Marines— and Chuck, who was already part of the Reserve Officer Training Corps (ROTC), was all ears.

Soon Colson walked into the Marine recruiting office. Behind a desk sat a tall recruiting first lieutenant named Cosgrove.

"I'd like to find out about joining the Marines," Colson told the officer.

"I think you're jumping the gun, Colson," Lieutenant Cosgrove said with a frown. "First, you've got to show us whether you're *good* enough for the Marine Corps."

Good enough? What does he mean by that? Colson wondered, his pride hurt. *I already rank pretty high in ROTC.* For the next few months,

Chuck Colson

he polished the brass buttons on his ROTC uniform and shined up his shoes. And every chance he got, Colson watched Lieutenant Cosgrove, trying to imitate his walk, his style.

One spring day, Colson found a typed notice on the bulletin board: "Colson report to Lieutenant Cosgrove." *Am I ready for this?* Colson wondered. *I'm not even sure I want to be in the Marines. Maybe I've just been trying to prove I'm good enough.*

As Chuck stood at attention in front of Lieutenant Cosgrove's desk, the officer twirled a pencil and scowled at the student officer. Then he suddenly stood up and said, "Colson, we think you're good enough."

That was all it took to resolve Chuck's indecision. He immediately said, "Sir, where do I sign up?"

Colson joined the Marines as soon as he graduated from Brown. *Semper Fidelis*—Always Faithful—is the slogan of the Marines. When the Marine symbol, a globe and anchor, was pinned on Chuck Colson's shoulders, he adopted the Marine slogan as his own. Devotion to country and faithfulness became essential parts of his life.

Chuck learned a lot in the Marines, and one of the things he learned was that he could push himself to do the impossible. One day at Camp

Quantico, Chuck proved that to himself. It was a hot and humid 103 degrees. Colson and his platoon were running through an obstacle course with full military packs, carrying their rifles. They made it through the course once and, between gasps for air, just as they were congratulating themselves on making it through without dying, they were ordered to run through it a second time. Many of them fainted during that second trip through the course—and Chuck was one of them.

When he woke up, he was lying on the ground with a Marine major standing over him. "Well, Colson," the officer growled. "If you can't keep up, somebody else will carry your rifle and pack for you."

Somebody else? Nobody else is going to carry my pack and rifle! Colson stumbled to his feet, grabbed his pack and rifle, and ran three miles back to the barracks. He didn't pass out again. He had pushed through an impossible barrier. He was a Marine.

*   *   *

One day Chuck's platoon shipped out for training exercises in the Caribbean, on Diegas Island. The Korean War had ended a few weeks earlier, so there would be no actual combat for

Chuck Colson

Always Tell the Truth

Colson and his platoon. Instead, they were given a training exercise on the island.

"There are two routes to your assigned destination!" the captain yelled. "Either a long, flat hike over smooth terrain"—he pointed in one direction "or the more direct approach—right there," and he pointed at the sheer cliff beside them. Colson stood at the bottom, staring straight up at sixty feet of rugged volcanic rock. "All right, men—up the cliff!" his captain ordered.

That's impossible, Colson thought. *Somebody, even me, might get killed climbing this—but hey, we're Marines.* So Chuck took a deep breath and charged ahead with the forty-five men in his platoon. With ropes and picks, they dug into the cliff and climbed their way to the top.

As Chuck stood beside his buddies at the top, the gentle breeze from the island blowing through his hair, he realized that his commander had been right. As a Marine, he could do the impossible. He could climb sheer cliffs and march incredible distances. Whatever it was, he could do it.

Besides building his self-confidence and encouraging him to push himself to his limits, the Marine Corps did something else for Chuck.

Chuck Colson

It reminded him of something his dad had taught him years before: "Whatever you do in life—it doesn't matter if it's cleaning toilets—do it well. Do it with excellence."

One Saturday morning, the gruff commander called for an inspection. As the leader of a platoon, Chuck was responsible to make sure his forty-five men had their material in perfect shape and everything shined. During the inspection, the men had to stand at attention. As the colonel finished, he turned to Colson and said, "Lieutenant, the toilets are dirty."

Colson snapped out a reply, "Yes sir. I'll have them cleaned."

"No," came the instant response. "Clean them yourself."

Chuck was amazed. *I'm an officer!* he thought. *Officers don't clean toilets!*

Then he remembered his dad's words about excellence. He changed into some work clothes and scrubbed those bathrooms until they were perfect. The commander had known what he was doing. For every inspection after that, Colson's men worked even harder. They didn't want to fail him again. And they never failed another inspection.

In the summer of 1954, Lieutenant Colson received orders: "Report at once with a seabag, an emergency." Within hours, he and his men were loaded onto an old World War II ship; soon they sailed for Guatemala, Central America. Their mission: to protect American lives in Guatemala.

As their ship glided through the sea that night, Colson stood on the deck. Everything around them was black except for the red-and-green lights from the other ships heading for Guatemala. Thousands of stars were scattered across the sky. It was about midnight, and Chuck found himself thinking about the forty-five men in his platoon. During the mission, he would be responsible for their lives. *Suppose some of us die,* he wondered. *What then? Is that the end? What's the purpose of all this?*

When Chuck was a boy, his parents had taken him to an Episcopal Sunday school, but nothing he'd heard or seen there had made much of an impression on him. Now, standing on the deck of a ship possibly heading into combat, Colson prayed a quick prayer—wondering not so much whether God was real but rather whether God had time to hear him.

Later that night the emergency was canceled, and the Marines returned to their base. He and his men had not been sent into combat after all. But the questions Chuck asked himself that

Chuck Colson

night had still not been answered, and years later, Chuck would find himself asking those same questions again.

Toward the end of his time in the Marines, Colson was sent to supply school. The school trained officers who ran the supply area of the Marines, something Chuck had no interest in. He wrote letters and tried to get his assignment changed to a different branch of the Marines. But no one listened. Despite his lack of interest, he graduated number one in his class at supply school. *Great*, Chuck thought, *just great. Now that I've graduated first in my class, they'll probably keep me in the supply area as long as I'm in the Marines. What's the point of that? If that's all I've got to look forward to, I should resign.*

And resign he did. Next stop: Washington, D.C.—the nation's capital.

Chuck Colson

2

A Taste of Politics

It was 1955—an exciting new day for America. Optimism was sweeping the country. Dwight Eisenhower, a famous general during World War II, had been elected president of the United States in 1952. Colson felt this new upbeat attitude as well. After completing his tour of duty in the Marines, he arrived in Washington, D.C., full of dreams and vision for the government, wanting to make his contribution.

Like his father, Chuck enrolled in a law school to take night classes. Then, along with eighty thousand other people, Chuck took an examination to get into an exclusive government program called the Junior Management Assistant Program. The program included classes in Washington, D.C., during the mornings and on-the-job training in the afternoons.

Chuck passed the written exam, performed well in a series of oral interviews, and finally was selected as one of the fifteen hundred young men to enter the program.

These young management trainees were allowed to select the government agency where they would receive their on-the-job training. Chuck chose the Navy Department. There, he was assigned to the printing office. On his first day, full of enthusiasm and high hopes, he walked into the office—and saw forty men sitting around drinking coffee and telling jokes.

What are these people doing? Colson wondered, finding his desk and taking a seat. *They're just wasting time! I won't be able to get anything done here—I want to be part of the solution, not part of the problem.*

After a few days of that, Chuck was fed up. He marched into the office of the director of the Junior Management Program and said, "I need a different job. It would be a waste of the government's money and my time to leave me in that printing office."

Chuck Colson

The director listened. He must have liked what he heard, because instead of firing Colson, he promoted him to a different position. But when Colson entered the office to start his new assignment, no one was working; everyone was sitting around drinking coffee and wasting time in small talk.

Chuck wasn't about to settle for that. He turned around and went back to the director and complained again.

After about four meetings with the director and four visits to time-wasting offices, Chuck was disgusted with the training program. Unless he landed a worthwhile job, he planned to find a job selling shoes somewhere and continue attending law school at night. Finally, Chuck ended up in the office of Raymond Folger, the assistant to the secretary of the Navy. Chuck told Mr. Folger about the different offices he had worked in, and how no one had seemed serious about his or her job; he explained how he had been through four different offices in only a few days and was beginning to lose hope in this special training program.

Raymond Folger listened to the young Colson. "Will you work for me?" he said, when Chuck had finished talking. "We could use someone like you in this office." Colson became the assistant to the assistant to the secretary of the Navy—a job usually reserved for someone with many years of government experience.

After a year in the Junior Management Program, Colson met Senator Leverett Saltonstall from his home state of Massachusetts. The grand old gentleman senator took a liking to Colson and hired him immediately to work in his Boston office. Senator Saltonstall was highly respected and skillful in his ability to negotiate with the lawmakers in Washington. But back home in Massachusetts, the Republican senator had neglected to strengthen his support. He was in danger of not being reelected.

The junior senator from Massachusetts, John F. Kennedy, was a rising star. Kennedy was a leading candidate for the Democratic presidential nomination.

Senator Saltonstall needed someone like Chuck Colson to get his office back on track. At age twenty-seven, Colson became the youngest administrative assistant in the Senate. He was a brash young man who knew the answers to any questions—and if he didn't, he pretended he did.

*   *   *

One day the vice president of the United

States, Richard Nixon, came to Boston to make a brief speech at a convention. Colson had been asked to write his speech; that gave Chuck a chance to meet Nixon for the first time. "That's very interesting," Nixon said as he read over the speech Colson had written. "That's very well done." But he pulled out his pen and began to change some of the sentences. After just a few minutes, he handed the speech back to Colson. "Here's that speech, Mr. Colson," the vice president said. "I appreciate your work on it."

Chuck quickly looked over the speech. It was totally revised! And it was one hundred percent improved.

Chuck recognized immediately the brilliance of the rewritten speech. During his work at Brown University and his years in Washington, D.C., Colson had been around some of the finest thinkers in the country—yet he had never seen anyone as sharp as Vice President Nixon. *Now there is an amazing mind,* Chuck thought.

*   *   *

As Senator Saltonstall headed into the election of 1960, he asked Chuck to manage his campaign. Saltonstall was running against the Democratic governor of Massachusetts, Foster Furcolo, the first Italian-American governor in the state. John F. Kennedy, the junior senator from Massachusetts, would be running for the presidential nomination. To Colson, it looked like an uphill battle for his boss.

Early in the campaign, Saltonstall fell far behind in the polls—about three hundred thousand votes. When Colson took charge of the campaign, his first move was to fire several people in the home office. That gave him a tough-guy reputation—and he ran the campaign in such a way that he kept that reputation. When it came to politics, Colson had learned every dirty trick in the book—such as tearing down the campaign posters of the opponents, or giving newspaper reporters false information that would smear his opponents.

Another campaign trick was to send out phony mailings about the opposing candidate. Colson sent out several of these phony mailings without his boss, Senator Saltonstall, knowing about it—and afterward, the polls began to shift. The Senator was gaining on his opponent.

In late September, Colson learned from a poll that Saltonstall was gaining popularity among Irish-American voters. If he could capture this large voting block for Saltonstall, Colson knew, it could turn the election in Saltonstall's favor.

Chuck Colson

Unknown to Senator Saltonstall, Colson rented a few rooms in a third-rate Boston hotel. First, he changed the locks on the doors at the hotel. Then he hired a number of young campaign workers and put them in those rooms with stacks of plain envelopes and a Boston telephone book. When they came across an Irish-sounding name, they addressed an envelope to that person. Their goal was to address over three hundred thousand envelopes. Into each envelope they stuffed a letter, signed by six well-known Irish Democrats, endorsing John F. Kennedy—a Democrat—for president and Saltonstall—a Republican—for senator. Though the two men were from different political parties, the letter discussed a variety of projects for Massachusetts that they had worked on together.

Senator Saltonstall didn't know about the letter or about Colson's plans to mail it to three hundred thousand Irish-Americans just before the election. In fact, in his campaign speeches, he supported the Republican Party's candidate for president—Richard Nixon.

On the Friday evening before election day, just before the mailing was ready to go out, Chuck stopped by the hotel hideaway. Although nearly exhausted from their impossible workload, twenty workers were still there, hand-stuffing the mounds of envelopes. They were nearly finished, and at midnight, they planned to load the stacks of letters into two station wagons and drive to a post office where a postmaster friendly to their cause had agreed to put the letters into the mail.

But there was a slight problem. Tom, a university freshman who was in charge of this project, asked to see Chuck alone. As they walked down the hallway, Tom said, "Chuck, one of the girls thinks we're being disloyal to Nixon. She threatened to run over to Republican Party headquarters and tell them about this mailing."

Colson shook his head. "That'll wreck everything. If people find out this letter came from the Saltonstall campaign, the whole thing will fail. It has to look like it came from Kennedy supporters. Nixon doesn't have a chance to win in this state anyway—not against Kennedy. I've told his people what we're doing. We're trying to keep a Republican in the Senate."

Colson walked in silence for a moment or two, thinking. Then he pulled out his wallet and gave Tom a hundred dollars in new ten-dollar bills. "Here's what we'll do, Tom. Take this girl out and get her drunk—or whatever it takes to keep her quiet until Election Day on Tuesday."

"No problem, Chuck," Tom said with a grin.

Chuck Colson

He was well known as a lady's man and was happy to follow Chuck's orders.

On Monday morning, three hundred thousand letters flooded into Irish homes across Massachusetts. The next day, Tuesday, these same voters marched to the polls and elected Kennedy and Saltonstall. Because the mailing had been carefully timed to arrive at the last minute, it was too late for Saltonstall's opponent to react to it or expose it.

The mailing and the senator's win earned Colson a reputation as a smooth political operator. Senator Saltonstall asked Chuck to stay on for six years as his administrative assistant, but Chuck turned him down. He was anxious to begin practicing law.

He still had a lot of interest in politics, though, and he had several political job offers to choose from. But he decided that working in government could wait until later.

His reputation in the law community had also grown, and several important Boston law firms offered Chuck a job. Instead, with five thousand dollars in his savings, Chuck joined a brilliant young lawyer named Charlie Morin. They opened two law offices—Morin in Boston and Chuck in Washington. Business boomed, and soon they had forty lawyers working in their firm.

As Chuck's law practice was growing, his family was growing too. After college, Chuck had married Nancy Billings, a girl from a well-known Boston family. They had three children—Wendell, Christian, and Emily. But first with Senator Saltonstall and then with his law firm, Chuck poured nearly all of his time and devotion into his work. His family received less and less of Chuck's attention until, in the early sixties, he separated from his wife. In 1964, his divorce became final.

Later that same year, Colson married one of the best-liked secretaries in Congress—Patty Hughes. A descendant of Irish immigrants, Patty had a zest for life. In the Army chapel next to Arlington Cemetery, they were married in a simple ceremony.

* * *

During his years in Boston, Chuck had several opportunities to meet with Richard Nixon. In 1964, Nixon asked Chuck to come to New York to advise him about running for president. Only four years earlier, Nixon had lost to John F. Kennedy. After Kennedy's assassination in 1963, Lyndon Johnson had become president,

Chuck Colson

and he would be the Democratic nominee. Barry Goldwater looked like the leading candidate for the Republican nomination.

Chuck sat with Nixon alone in the corner office on the twenty-fourth floor of a building in New York. "You're the only one who can save the Republican Party from a sure loss, Mr. Nixon," Chuck said. "You should run for the presidency."

Nixon's eyes lit with excitement as he thought about another campaign. "Johnson would have to debate me, wouldn't he, Chuck?" Nixon recalled debating Kennedy four years earlier, and he knew that Johnson would face pressure to debate.

But when he considered the odds against him, Nixon shook his head. "It will be tough to get the nomination this year," Nixon said, staring out at the New York skyline. "Well, if not this time, there's always next time."

Barry Goldwater won the Republican nomination, and as Colson had predicted, he lost in November to Johnson in a landslide. The Republican Party would have to wait four more years.

In 1968, it was Richard Nixon who won the Republican nomination, and Chuck took a leave of absence from his law firm to work for Nixon's presidential campaign. He told his law partners, "The country needs Nixon now. I'll be back with you after the election."

When Nixon won the presidency that year, Chuck received several offers of political jobs in Washington. His old friend, John Volpe, former governor of Massachusetts, joined Nixon's cabinet as secretary of transportation. Volpe offered Chuck a top position in his department. Another friend from Chuck's college days at Brown University, Elliot Richardson, became Nixon's undersecretary of State. Richardson called Chuck and asked him to serve as an assistant secretary. It was a tempting offer, but Chuck turned it down. If he was going to work in government, he wanted to work for Nixon himself.

Late in the fall of 1969, Chuck got an invitation to come to the White House. A Navy commander in full-dress military uniform showed Chuck through the White House. They walked toward a section of the hallway that looked like a plain, white-plastered wall. But as he got closer, Chuck realized that the wall contained a hidden door. It was a private door to the Oval Office—the office of the president of the United States.

Chuck walked through that door into a sun-filled room; he walked across the blue-and-gold, oval rug with the Great Seal of the United States in the middle, matching the white plaster seal in the ceiling. Near the large windows overlooking the south lawn of the White House, the president sat behind a large mahogany desk.

President Nixon was studying a brown leather folder, a pair of reading glasses perched on his nose. It was the first time Chuck had ever seen the president using reading glasses.

Nixon looked up and smiled. "Good to see you again, Chuck. I'll be finished in a minute. Have a seat, boy." Chuck noticed that the brown notebook had letters across the front: "Daily Intelligence Summary. The President."

It had been several years since Chuck had first met Richard Nixon, but this was the first time he had spoken with Nixon as the president of the United States. It was not to be the last. As they sat together that morning, alone in that Oval Office, the president of the United States asked Colson, at age thirty-eight, to become Nixon's special counsel.

Because of his upbringing and because of the lessons he'd learned in the Marines, Chuck had a highly developed sense of duty. *The president needs you,* the little voice in his head told him. *It's your duty. You have to accept this position.* So Chuck Colson left his job with the law firm where he earned about two hundred thousand dollars a year and took a White House job that paid forty thousand dollars a year—special counsel to the president of the United States.

One day not long after that, Chuck was in his new office in the White House, looking out over the south lawn. He thought back to the lessons he had learned from his dad on those Sunday afternoons on the porch steps: *That's part of the dream of living in America. If you work hard, if you put your mind to it, you can succeed, you can get to the top.*

It's true, Chuck thought, *You can work hard in America and get to the top. Here I am, Chuck Colson, in the halls of power of the White House.*

He took a deep breath and shook his head. *So why do I feel so empty inside?* he wondered.

Chuck Colson

3

Hatchet Man for the President

Beep! The little radio receiver on Chuck Colson's belt demanded his attention. Everyone in that Capitol building meeting room turned and looked at him. As the special counsel for the thirty-seventh president of the United States, Richard Nixon, Colson spent much of his time in meetings such as this one with leaders of Congress.

"Excuse me a moment," Chuck said. Lifting the device to his ear, he heard, "Colson, Colson, report to the White House operator." He left the meeting immediately to find a phone.

"The president wants to see you right away in his office," the White House operator said.

Power. It came with the office of the president, and Colson was one of Nixon's closest associates and most passionate supporters. That support had earned Colson a reputation: He was willing to do whatever it took—even if "whatever it took" was questionable—to promote the president and his policies.

A *Wall Street Journal* headline in the fall of 1971 described that reputation: "Nixon Hatchet Man . . . Chuck Colson Handles President's Dirty Work." In the news story that followed, a staff member from a senator's office was quoted: "Colson would walk over his own grandmother if he had to." At the time, Colson joked with his staff about the headline.

Hatchet man. The president gave Colson the jobs that had to get done at any cost, because he knew that Colson would get them done. Some people considered his methods underhanded, maybe even against the law—despite his training as a lawyer. To serve Nixon, Chuck would take almost any risk.

Colson's limousine sped past the government buildings in downtown Washington, D.C.

In the backseat, Chuck pored over memos and government paperwork. As the car drove up to the tall metal gates of the White House, he barely noticed. A blue-suited officer saluted, checked Colson's identification, and waved him through.

Inside, agents nodded and gave him permission to enter the White House briefing room. Colson found Nixon and his twelve senior aides gathered. Secretary of State Henry Kissinger, obviously upset, was pacing the room.

"There can be no foreign policy in this government until this is taken care of!" he ranted. "We might just as well turn it all over to the Soviets and get it over with."

"What is it?" Colson asked the president quietly as he took his seat.

"It's these leaks again, Chuck," the president began. Inwardly, Colson groaned. Not again. For some time now, someone in government had been giving secret information to the press. The president's staff had been unable to find out who was leaking that information, and thus plug the leak. And the publication of this information in the press was interfering with secret negotiations between the United States and Moscow, and also between the United States and Vietnam.

"These leaks are slowly and systematically

destroying us!" Kissinger shouted. He slammed his fist on the antique table. Pencils scattered and coffee cups rattled. "Destroying us!"

Chuck had seen Kissinger, who looked like a typical university professor, get angry in other meetings. His glasses would bounce up and down on his face as it got red. Normally, Kissinger's fits of temper would pass quickly. But not this time. Chuck had never seen anything like it.

As Kissinger raved on, Chuck began to get the picture. A newspaper article from the day before in the *New York Times* had set Kissinger off. The article was the first in a series of stories called the Pentagon Papers.

Colson had read the article himself—it contained a bunch of old memos and telegraph cables, all from people who had worked for the government years before under former president Kennedy. The documents were about how the U.S. had entered the Vietnam War.

Kissinger turned to Bob Haldeman, the president's chief of staff, and said, "I tell you, Bob, the president must act—today!" He went on to explain that, although the information in this first article wasn't that damaging in itself, the timing was terrible—these stories in the newspapers could break down secret negotiations with Moscow and Vietnam.

"Look at this!" the secretary of state said as he passed around three pieces of paper. "Cables from Australia, Great Britain, and Canada. They can't trust us! Why should they? If countries that we count as our friends can't trust us to keep a secret, how can our enemies, like the Russians and the Chinese?"

As the discussion continued, the Justice Department raised additional concerns: If this type of information was released, CIA agents who worked in other countries might be identified, endangering their lives and costing the United States an important source for gathering information and defending the country. As Colson listened, his concern grew. Even the old information in these articles could influence today's events.

The source of the information in these articles was Daniel Ellsberg. A former employee of Henry Kissinger, Ellsberg had created these plans about Vietnam. When he left government service, Ellsberg kept copies of many secret documents, and now he was releasing them to the public. This was his way of protesting the Vietnam War. Almost overnight, Ellsberg became a champion and hero to the Americans

Hatchet Man for the President   47

who opposed the war in Vietnam. But the FBI reports that the attorney general related to Nixon, Colson, and rest of this key group at the White House indicated that Ellsberg belonged to a Communist spy group.

President Nixon saw Ellsberg as an enemy to be silenced. "I want him exposed, Chuck," Nixon said, bringing the discussion to a close. "I want the truth about him known. I don't care how you do it. We're going to let the country know what kind of 'hero' Mr. Ellsberg is." Nixon paused a second and then added in a stern tone, "Do you understand me? That's an order."

"Yes, sir. It will be done," Chuck replied. It didn't take much to encourage him to go after Ellsberg. As a former Marine, Colson had friends fighting in Vietnam, risking their lives every day. To him, Ellsberg was not a peacemaker but rather a roadblock in the efforts for peace.

Following the president's orders, Colson told his staff to nail Ellsberg in the newspapers and magazines. A few days later, a reporter digging into Ellsberg's background asked Chuck some questions. Glad for the opportunity, Colson gave the reporter some information that was very damaging to Ellsberg's reputation—information that came from secret FBI documents.

Colson's campaign against Ellsberg was somewhat successful. The newspapers agreed not to print the most sensitive documents. Discussions with the Soviets and Chinese continued—but here at home, the damage had been done to Nixon's reputation. The public grew discontent with his performance, and his popularity fell to a new low. And, to the immense frustration of Nixon and his staff, that public discontent continued to be fueled by new leaks of sensitive information.

As the days passed, Nixon's low popularity and the growing antiwar publicity wore on the president. Late one evening, the president told Haldeman and Colson, "I don't care how it's done—I want these leaks *stopped!* Don't give me any excuses! Use any means!" The president slapped the table. "Bob," he said to Haldeman, "I want results—and I want them now! Find the person you need to stop these leaks, and hire him!"

That late-night discussion marked a change in the president. From that time on, he was willing to go beyond the normal methods, beyond the accepted methods, to accomplish his goal. He was, like Colson, willing to do whatever it took. Months later, the importance of this turning point would become clear.

Chuck Colson

The man hired to silence Ellsberg and stop the leaks was an ex-CIA agent, E. Howard Hunt. Colson assigned Hunt a tiny cubicle on the third floor of the Executive Office building.

Hunt's performance on his first assignment gave Colson cause for concern. Hunt was to interview a CIA agent who had some information for the president. A secret-service agent hid a tape recorder under part of a sofa to record the interview. But Hunt sat on the recorder and broke it, so he didn't get any recorded information. That gave Chuck a hint of how poorly Hunt would do his job.

A few weeks later, Hunt teamed up with an ex-FBI agent—G. Gordon Liddy. Colson and other White House insiders called the team "the plumbers" and gave them broad powers to plug any sensitive leaks of information.

Later that summer, Hunt and Liddy broke into the offices of a psychiatrist in Los Angeles where Daniel Ellsberg had been a patient. The plumbers were looking for Ellsberg's private records at the doctor's office.

*   *   *

"Colson! Get over to my office—immediately!" press secretary Ron Ziegler yelled into the phone.

"I'll be there right away, Ron," Chuck said. As he set down the phone, he let out a soft chuckle. He knew why Ziegler was angry.

The newspapers had been running many articles about Chuck, many of them very negative and based on questionable sources. Chuck was growing more and more upset with the reporters. But he could do nothing about it because he was under strict orders from Ziegler not to talk with the press.

To vent his frustration, Chuck had drafted a memo to a reporter at the *New York Times* and sent the copy to Ziegler, who had blown his top when he read it—as Chuck had known he would.

As Colson walked into the press secretary's office, Ziegler tore into him. "Chuck—you're going to destroy our reputation sending memos like this to the press! Why did you do it? You know I didn't want this sort of thing to—"

With a laugh, Colson held up his hand and interrupted Ziegler. "It's a joke, Ron. Relax. I wrote the memo and sent you the copy—but here's the original." Colson pulled the document out of a file folder. "I never sent it."

Even in the White House, even under stress, Colson's love for practical jokes continued.

*   *   *

In January, President Nixon began his campaign for reelection. Because of the damage to Nixon's reputation due to the Ellsberg leaks, the early polls showed him in a close race with Democratic front-runner Edmund Muskie. Nixon's campaign needed a boost—a good dose of the old slug-'em-in-the-gut politics that Chuck had learned years before.

By late January, the president was certain that the secret negotiations with the North Vietnamese were not going to be successful, so he decided that he had little to lose by going public about the negotiations. On national TV, Nixon stunned the nation by announcing that for the past thirty months, Kissinger had been shuttling between the U.S. and Paris to make generous peace offers to the Vietnamese.

Surprised at the announcement, Muskie flew to Washington the next day and spoke to an antiwar group, denouncing the president's peace efforts.

Attorney General John Mitchell, who was just about to take over the management of President Nixon's reelection campaign, told Colson and the others in the White House to ignore Muskie's response to the president's announcement. He believed that any attack on

Muskie would only hurt Nixon and help Muskie in the election.

But both Nixon and Colson believed otherwise. Even though secretaries of state normally stay out of election politics, Chuck asked then-Secretary of State Bill Rogers to accuse Muskie of wrecking the United States peace talks.

The next morning, Rogers made a surprise statement, charging that Muskie had undercut the bargaining power of the United States to end the Vietnam War. Attorney General Mitchell, angered that his instructions had been ignored, somehow got wind that Chuck had been behind this attack on Muskie. In a rage, he telephoned Colson and said, "I'm going to the president unless you promise never to attack Muskie again." Colson promised—after all, he didn't think he would need to attack Muskie again.

And he was right. After Rogers' statement, Muskie's popularity dropped like a lead balloon. A new candidate began to lead the Democratic Party—George McGovern.

Everything was in place now for a landslide reelection for President Nixon. Neither Chuck Colson nor anyone else on the president's team had any idea how much turmoil the months ahead would hold.

Chuck Colson

4

The Pressure Builds—Watergate

On a hot afternoon in June 1972, Chuck Colson sat by the pool in his backyard. He was just thinking about diving in for a quick swim when the phone rang. It was the White House. Chuck immediately recognized the voice of Nixon's chief domestic aide, John Ehrlichman. "Chuck, have you heard from your friend Howard Hunt lately?" Ehrlichman asked.

"He doesn't work at the White House anymore, John," Colson answered. "I think he's on the Reelection Committee for the president. Why?"

"Could be a problem," Ehrlichman answered. "There was a break-in at Democratic headquarters over at the Watergate building. They caught the burglars, and one of them had something in his pocket with Hunt's name on it. That's it so far—I'll get back to you if anything else happens."

Colson put the phone down uneasily. Hunt. He had known that name would come back to haunt him. Just a few months before, Howard Hunt had come by his office with some sort of intelligence plan. Hunt hadn't given any of the details—*but I sure hope this robbery wasn't part of it,* Colson worried.

But by early the next week, the media had made the connection. One of the men who had broken into the Democratic headquarters had worked for Howard Hunt, and since in recent months Hunt had worked for Chuck Colson, the newspapers were tying "Nixon's Hatchet Man," Chuck Colson, to the Watergate break-in.

That afternoon, President Nixon called Chuck into the Oval Office and told him to ignore the stories. "It's me they're after, Chuck," the president said.

And that became the White House attitude

Chuck Colson

toward the story: It was a a minor distraction, an insignificant indiscretion being blown out of proportion by the media.

And Colson had plenty of other things to occupy his attention. He and all of his staff were right in the middle of a presidential election, and Colson wanted to make sure that Nixon won it. Hours were long—twelve to sixteen hours regularly—for both Colson and his staff. Papers and coffee cups were strewn across desks; meals were eaten in the office with a phone in one hand. Everything was a rush. Only half-joking, Colson wrote a memo to his staff canceling all vacations and instructing everyone to work seven days a week for the next two-and-a-half months. "Last week's UPI story said that I would walk over my grandmother [to reelect the president] if necessary," Colson's memo read. "That was absolutely accurate."

For the president, Colson would do practically anything.

And what he did, worked. In November of 1972, Colson stood by, exhausted but exhilarated, as a grinning Richard Nixon raised his hands in the familiar two-fingered "victory" salute before a cheering crowd of election workers (and a battery of television cameras) to acknowledge his reelection.

For Colson, it was a bittersweet victory. It was also his farewell to the White House. He had told the president months earlier that, no matter who won the election, Colson planned to return to law practice afterward.

A few days later, Nixon accepted Colson's letter of resignation as special counsel. Nixon wrote: "I shall always cherish your loyal friendship and in equal measure, I shall always treasure the superb work you did for our party, our Administration and the people of this good land."

Colson boarded the plane to Boston, took his seat, and sat glumly staring at the newspaper he wasn't even interested in reading. *Something must be wrong with me*, he thought. *I've only been back practicing law for a few weeks, and already I'm bored with it. I've got no zeal, no competitive drive. I'm just going through the motions.*

The furor about Watergate wasn't helping, either. Nixon had been wrong; Watergate wasn't turning out to be an insignificant distraction at all. The media had continued to dig, and the country seemed to want answers. The story dominated television and the newspapers, and Colson's name appeared in those stories regularly. In fact, some reporters seemed to feel that the primary responsibility for the break-in lay with Colson. Now, a Senate committee was investigating the break-in, and a grand jury was meeting. It was getting worse rather than better, and Colson was worried.

He was going to Boston to handle some legal matters for an old customer, the Raytheon Company, a large electronics firm. Chuck had worked with Raytheon before his days in the White House. He spent the day meeting with company executives. Then, just before he left, he was told that Tom Phillips, the company president, wanted to meet with him.

"How long has it been since you've seen Tom?" asked one of the executives.

"Four years," Colson answered.

The man nodded. Then he said, "I ought to warn you, then. He's changed. He's had a religious experience."

A religious experience? Colson remembered Tom Phillips as a hard worker, an aggressive businessman. Tom had become an engineer for Raytheon when he was twenty-five, just one of fifty thousand employees. But by the time he was thirty-six, Phillips was an executive vice president for the company. He had climbed to the top—the hard way. If he became soft now because of some religious experience, he'd have a hard time leading a major company in a competitive marketplace.

As Colson walked into Phillips' office, he noticed a peace about the man. *I wouldn't mind finding a little peace myself,* he thought grimly. *This Watergate business is about to tear me apart.*

Near the end of their friendly discussion, Colson said, "Tom, you've changed. What's happened to you?"

Tom smiled and said, "Yes, I *have* changed, Chuck. I've accepted Jesus Christ and committed my life to him."

Colson felt uneasy; he shifted in his chair. He'd never heard anyone talk that way before. For Colson, Jesus Christ was a historical figure, but this important businessman spoke as if Christ were alive in the here and now. Colson changed the subject—but the thought nagged at his mind: *Could I find the same peace?*

Shaking hands as Colson left, Phillips said, "Let's get together again soon, Chuck, to talk about this some more." And Colson made a mental note: *Make time in my schedule for another meeting with Tom Phillips.*

*   *   *

As the Watergate investigation intensified

and suspicions about Colson increased, Chuck turned to his law partner, Dave Shapiro, for advice.

"Take a lie-detector test, Chuck," Shapiro suggested. "It might keep the prosecutors off your back."

"A lie-detector test? I'm not about to trust my reputation to some kind of black magic," Colson protested. "I don't trust those things, and I don't trust the quacks who run them." Although he felt that he had nothing to hide and would tell the truth, Chuck worried that, because his nerves were shot from all the attention about him in the news, he would be too nervous to pass the test.

But after he'd thought about it for several days, he agreed to go to New York and take the test. He caught the last flight out from Washington that night and arrived in New York during a drenching rainstorm.

As he walked into Richard Arther's office for the test, Shapiro came out with Arther. "You look worried, Chuck," Shapiro said to his friend. "Don't be. Even if you fail the test, I'll still represent you. Whether you are guilty or innocent, I'll still win your case."

What hope do I have if even my own lawyer doesn't believe I'm innocent of any involvement in this Watergate mess? Colson wondered in frustration.

At Arther's direction, Colson sat down in a dentist-like chair to "wire-up" for the test. Arther wired each of Chuck's fingertips; the wires led to a metal box. Then Arther sat, adjusted his equipment, and was ready to begin.

"Tell me every lie that you've ever told," Arther said.

"You must be kidding," Chuck replied. "We'd be here all day."

Arther shook his head. "No, I'm serious. It's important that the test begin with a clean slate. We need to raise these issues from your past and get them out of the way."

Those preliminary questions took an hour. As they talked, a machine made squiggly lines on a long sheet of paper in response to the information it picked up from the wires on Chuck's fingertips. Arther could tell by the pattern of those lines whether a person was answering the questions honestly or dishonestly.

Finally, Arther asked Colson six critical questions, such as: "Did you order the Watergate break-in?"

"No."

"Did you know about the break-in in advance?"

"No."

Finally the ordeal was over. *I failed it,* Colson thought. *I just know it.*

"I'll have to study this before we know anything," Arther said as he looked at the long sheet of paper with squiggly lines.

"Why don't you stick around, Chuck?" Dave Shapiro encouraged him. "Let's wait together for the results."

"No, I've got to catch the next train back to Washington," Chuck said and grabbed his coat to leave. "Call me when you find out."

On the street, the rain drenched Colson as he tried to flag down a taxi. He was so numb from the testing and from the stress of the past few months that he didn't care what the rain did to his clothes. Finally, a taxi saw him and pulled over.

"Chuck! Chuck, stop!" yelled a voice. Colson turned and saw Dave Shapiro running out of the building. "We've got the results! In fact, Dick double-checked them. You passed the test with flying colors! No doubt about it—you're telling the truth, and we can prove it."

Despite the rain, as the two men hugged on a busy street corner in New York, tears ran down Colson's cheeks. At last—someone believed he was telling the truth.

*   *   *

By late summer, public interest in Watergate had grown so strong that the Watergate hearings in the Senate were televised every day. Americans gathered around their TV sets and watched the drama unfold. One day, one of Bob Haldeman's deputies made a startling statement—all of the president's meetings in the Oval Office had been secretly taped since 1971.

Like so many others, Colson and Shapiro were watching the hearings when the news broke about the secret tapes. At first, Dave looked suspiciously at his friend and client.

"Dave, I don't know anything about these tapes," Chuck said, shocked and frightened at this unexpected news. "I'm hearing this for the first time, just like you."

When Chuck saw the look in Dave's eyes change from suspicion to sympathy, he knew that Dave shared his fears that these tapes could hurt him.

"I thought Nixon was supposed to be your friend," Dave said. "Some friend."

Chuck wasn't sure what to feel. At first he felt shock that all of those supposedly private conversations had actually been taped and now would probably be made public. Next he felt relief—those tapes should prove that he had known nothing about the Watergate break-in. Then worry—the tapes would just add fuel to the fire of public outrage about Watergate.

As the televised Watergate hearings continued, the work of government came to a halt. In nearly every government office, there was a television surrounded by public employees watching the Senate hearings with intense interest. What could they learn next? Chuck had been involved in government in one way or another for twenty years, and he had never seen anything like these brutal hearings. And the longer it went on, the more empty and discouraged he felt. Was this all there was to life?

Chuck thought about going to see Tom Phillips. He remembered the feeling of peace that Tom had seemed to give off, like a glow. Chuck's life was totally consumed now with Watergate, and all it was bringing him was fear, worry, and pain.

Every day, the tension in the capital increased, and with it, media interest in Nixon's Hatchet Man. Most mornings, the Colsons woke up to find reporters and photographers camped on their doorstep. Chuck and Patty felt that they needed to escape the suspicion and publicity, and they arranged to spend a few days at a cottage on the Maine coast.

On the way, they stopped in Boston to see Chuck's parents. But Chuck didn't stay there long. "I've got some business to take care of," he told Patty, and drove off. Late-night meetings and long working hours had been such a normal part of Chuck's life for years that Patty didn't even ask where he was headed.

Even so, Chuck felt a little guilty for leaving Patty behind. After all, it was the beginning of a vacation and a Sunday evening. But Chuck had made an appointment to see Tom Phillips, and he wasn't about to miss it. He was too anxious to find out more about Tom's religious experience. What made him so different?

On a quiet street, Chuck pulled into the long driveway of the Phillips house—a large New England colonial home.

Thinking it was the front door, Chuck knocked on the door nearest the driveway. It turned out to be the door to their kitchen. With a smile, Gert Phillips opened the door and greeted Chuck warmly. They had just finished supper.

"I'll get Tom—he's playing tennis with the children," she said. Almost immediately, Tom arrived with his nineteen-year-old daughter,

Debby, and sixteen-year-old son, Tommy. Gert fixed everyone tall glasses of ice tea.

Tom led Chuck through the house to a porch with large, screened windows. Since it was unusually hot and humid for New England, Tom persuaded Chuck to take off his suit coat, and finally even his tie.

"Are you okay, Chuck?" Tom asked. It was the same question Tom had asked to start their earlier conversation back in March. And with the Watergate investigation constantly in the news, it was a fair question. It was also a question that Chuck avoided.

He shrugged. "I'm getting a bit worn down from this Watergate business. But I'd prefer to talk about you, Tom. I knew you several years ago, and now you're different. Tell me what happened to you—because, whatever it is, I want to know about it."

So Tom told Chuck the story of his life— how he had worked hard to get ahead in his company and become one of its leaders. That success had brought him many things—a big home, fancy cars, every material thing a person could want. Even so, he would wake up in the night and look at the stars and wonder how to find a personal relationship with God.

One day, in New York, Tom attended a Billy

Graham Crusade. He sat in the upper part of the stadium, high above the platform where Billy Graham preached. But he could still hear everything the preacher said: that Jesus was more than just a historical figure—that he was, in fact, the living God. At the end of his message, when Graham asked those who wanted to receive Jesus Christ as their personal Savior to come down to the front, Tom Phillips, along with hundreds of others, gave his life to Christ. "And from that day on, Chuck," Tom explained, "my life has been changed.

"Chuck, there's a book that has meant a lot to me. It's called *Mere Christianity*, by C. S. Lewis," Tom said. "Lewis was a university professor in England and a student of the Bible. I'd like to read a chapter from this book to you, Chuck, and I think you'll see why I like it."

Then Tom read the chapter called, "The Great Sin, Pride." The words struck Chuck with incredible power. He couldn't deny it—selfish pride filled every aspect of his life. He was living only for himself, and he had hurt many other people to get what he wanted. Now he was paying the price.

"The Lord can change your life, Chuck." Tom said. "Will you pray with me?"

What do I do now? Chuck wondered, a little

embarrassed. *I've never prayed with anyone else, except when someone prays at a meal or in church. I'm not sure I could pray in someone's living room.*

So he answered, "No, but I'll listen as you pray."

Tom's prayers were unlike anything Chuck had ever experienced. He simply talked with God. He didn't use any of the formal language, the "thees" and "thous" that Chuck associated with prayer. It was like a conversation with a best friend. Then, after a long period of silence, Tom said, "Amen."

Tom then gave Chuck a copy of *Mere Christianity*. "I encourage you to read through the rest of it, Chuck. There are many valuable lessons here, and much wisdom," he said.

At the kitchen door, the two men said good-bye. *I wish I could find that kind of peace,* Chuck thought as he walked back to his car, tears welling up in his eyes.

He climbed into his car and shut the door, but the real meaning of what Tom had said suddenly struck him with fresh power. He was so overcome that he couldn't get his keys into the ignition to start the car, couldn't pull out of the driveway because he couldn't see for all the tears in his eyes and streaming down his cheeks.

To his amazement, Chuck found himself crying and calling out to God with the first honest prayer of his life. Over and over, Chuck said, "Take me as I am. Take me as I am."

The tough guy from the White House—the ex-Marine captain, Nixon's Hatchet Man—had found a personal relationship with Jesus Christ.

5

Confession
and Prison

After his emotional evening with Tom
Phillips, Chuck and Patty cruised up the Maine
coast, leaving Washington, D.C., Watergate, and
the media pressure farther and farther behind.
They settled into a little cottage motel by the sea
and tried to relax. With a yellow legal pad in his
lap, Chuck started to think about the decision
he had made to follow Christ, occasionally jot-
ting down a few notes.

He thought, in fact, about most of his life up

to that point, taking a break now and then to read the Bible or to pray and talk with Patty. Chuck was no stranger to deep thought, but in the past he'd thought mostly about himself— how to avoid prison, how to protect himself, how to prove his innocence. Now he began to think about some of the others involved in Watergate. What about Daniel Ellsberg, for example—the man who turned over the Pentagon Papers to the reporters? Part of Chuck still disliked Ellsberg. Releasing those papers to the press had been very wrong, Chuck felt. Still, Chuck had authorized a secret effort to damage Ellsberg's reputation. Men from the White House had broken into a doctor's office in Los Angeles and stolen Ellsberg's medical records. Even Daniel Ellsberg, Chuck reluctantly admitted to himself, had rights—and weren't those rights more important than preserving secrets of the United States government? With surprise, Chuck realized that Christ was changing his view of the world. For the first time, he began to question his role in Watergate and in the Nixon administration.

Toward the end of his vacation, staring out at the ocean, Chuck began to pray: *Lord Jesus, I believe you. I accept you. Please come into my life. I commit it to you.* The waves beat against the shore. Chuck could almost feel the fears and the hate that had been so much a part of his life for so many years draining away.

With a smile, he picked up his pad to write a letter to Tom Phillips telling him about his new relationship with God.

*　　*　　*

A friend of Tom's, Doug Coe, who spent much of his time setting up and participating in meetings with Christians in government, came to Chuck's law office in Washington. As the two men talked, they found out that they knew many of the same people.

"By the way, Chuck, you'll want to meet with Senator Harold Hughes," Doug suggested. "He's a tremendous Christian."

Chuck laughed. "Harold Hughes? No way! Harold Hughes can't stand me! He's anti-Nixon and anti-Colson. We're way apart politically."

"Politics doesn't matter here," Doug said. "You and Harold are brothers in Christ. You're a Christian now, Chuck, and that means you have men and women across this city who'll want to help you."

Chuck shook his head. He'd love to believe that—but could he? For months, his life had been one huge battlefield. He'd been dodging reporters camped on his front lawn, fighting lawyers who were digging into the charges from Watergate, and speaking before committees of Congress who were investigating the problems in Nixon's administration. And if *anyone* would want to help him, the least likely person would be Senator Harold Hughes!

"Okay, Doug, try to set it up if you want to," Chuck said. "But I doubt that Senator Hughes will meet with me."

A few weeks later, Doug pulled up in front of Chuck's office to pick him up for a meeting. There was someone else in the car, Chuck noticed. As he climbed into the backseat of the battered Chevy station wagon, he recognized the other person—Harold Hughes, his long-time enemy.

Senator Hughes, who has deep-set eyes and an American Indian-like appearance, was casually dressed. The men made small talk until they reached the colonial suburban home of Al Quie, the congressman from Minnesota.

A small group—including Chuck's wife, Patty, who had also come—sat around the Quie house talking for a while. Finally Harold Hughes turned to Colson. "They say you've met Jesus Christ, Chuck," Senator Hughes said. "How about telling us about it?" The room grew quiet, and everyone turned to look at Chuck.

Chuck glanced uncomfortably around the room. Tell a whole roomful of strangers about the most personal decision of his life? It felt so strange. Slowly, Chuck told the story of his evening with Tom Phillips, his prayer to Jesus Christ, and the changes now taking place in his life. As he talked, Chuck felt the acceptance and love from the other people in the room.

When he finished, Senator Hughes said, "That's all I need to know, Chuck. Jesus has forgiven you, and now you're my brother in Christ. I'll stand with you in the days ahead." Then Harold threw his arms around Chuck and hugged him. *Amazing!* Chuck thought. *With the love of Jesus, even former enemies can become close friends.*

*   *   *

"What if the reporters find out you're a Christian?" Patty asked one day several weeks later as she and Chuck sat at their kitchen table. "Will it help you or hurt you?"

"Probably hurt me," he said. He had thought about that question quite a bit. "But it's none of their business, and I have no plans to tell them."

Chuck's decision to follow Christ had been

a private decision, and he planned for it to stay that way. He hadn't told many of his best friends, or even family members. And why should anyone else care?

He was soon to find out that others *did* care.

Months earlier, when Chuck had worked in the White House, his workday had begun shortly after eight in the morning when the men of power, including the president, met around a table in the Roosevelt Room and talked about important topics. Chuck hadn't known then that, twice a month, down in the White House basement, a different kind of meeting was taking place at the same time: A small group of people who worked in the White House would meet for prayer.

But now that Chuck was a Christian, Harold Hughes brought him to one of those breakfast prayer meetings. During the breakfast, the senator from Iowa told the small group about his relationship with Jesus Christ. Chuck and the others listened. At the end of the talk, Senator Hughes asked Chuck to close the meeting in prayer.

With his head bowed, Chuck prayed: "Jesus, help each of us—no matter what position we have in government. Without your hand

Chuck Colson

on us, Lord, we can't possibly serve the country. We ask these things in Jesus' name. Amen."

The men at that meeting rose and surrounded Chuck and warmly welcomed him. He had served in government for many years, but never had he felt as appreciated as he did that morning.

Later that day, Jerry Warren, the assistant press secretary in the White House, held a news conference. He planned to make a routine announcement about a new law that President Nixon would sign that day.

During the conference, Dan Rather from CBS News asked, "Jerry, why is the president continuing to see Charles Colson?"

"I don't think he is," Jerry said.

"Well, why was Colson at the White House today?" Rather asked.

After a short pause, Jerry said, "He was attending a prayer breakfast that the staff has every other week."

Prayer breakfast. Laughter roared through the room. No one believed that Nixon's Hatchet Man would be even remotely interested in prayer. As soon as the press conference was over, the reporters raced to the phones to call in this new story about Watergate for tomorrow's newspapers and television broadcasts. Many of the reporters called Chuck at his Washington law office to ask him about his decision to follow Christ. In simple and clear terms, Chuck explained his newfound faith—and mentally said good-bye to the idea of keeping this decision private.

During the next month, the political cartoonists of the newspapers loved to draw Chuck Colson in a monk's habit out in front of the White House. In one cartoon, he was tacking up a big sign that said, "Repent!" Few in the media or in government took his declaration of faith seriously; few believed that a tough guy like Chuck Colson could change. More likely it was a ploy to get a lighter sentence if he should be convicted, they thought. And even if the changes were real, would they last?

*   *   *

The summer dragged on with court appearances and testifying before committees in Congress. In between, Chuck gave a few talks at prayer breakfasts about his newfound faith in Jesus and made a few media appearances. It was while he was being interviewed on *60 Minutes* that Chuck said, as he had often said before, "In my own heart, I'm innocent of most of the things they're accusing me of—"

Chuck Colson

He stopped talking, forgetting the television cameras and microphones, suddenly struck by what he had just said. His mind raced. "Innocent of *most* of these things," he had said. In that few seconds of silence, he made an important decision: to plead guilty to something he *was* guilty of—the spreading of false information about Daniel Ellsberg. Chuck had given newspaper reporters information about Ellsberg that wasn't true.

Chuck discussed that decision with some of his new Christian friends and with Patty. Then he asked Dave Shapiro, who was still representing him, to talk with the Watergate prosecutors.

Shapiro tried to talk him out of it. "Chuck, you're crazy. You'll never practice law again, and you'll go to prison."

"No, Dave, I'm not crazy," Chuck said. "Calm down. Just tell the prosecutors that I want to tell the truth."

When Chuck and his lawyers met with the Watergate prosecutors, the prosecutors were eager to accept Colson's confession. They were willing to drop all other charges if Chuck would plead guilty to spreading false information about Ellsberg. In fewer than ten minutes, the judge had recorded and accepted Chuck Colson's guilty plea. Sentencing would be in three weeks.

Judge Gesell would have to decide whether Chuck would have to pay a fine, serve time in prison, or both.

That three weeks allowed some of Chuck's friends to show their support by asking the judge to show mercy and give Chuck a light sentence.

Bill Maloney, Chuck's fraternity brother from Brown University who had become a Marine, was one of these friends. Bill had made a career for himself in the Marines and was now a general. But General Maloney was willing to risk his military future for a friend, and he made an appointment to see Chuck's probation officer.

The rows of medals he had received for service during the Korean War looked impressive on General Maloney's uniform as he walked in and sat down to speak with the probation officer. "No matter where Chuck Colson is, he will be successful," the general said. "If Colson was selling apples from a cart in front of the Washington Monument, I'd like to have a part of that business, because I know it would succeed." Then he recommended that the court show Chuck mercy.

Other friends and former law clients wrote letters of support to Judge Gesell, recommending a light sentence for Chuck.

On June 21, Chuck and Dave Shapiro stood before the judge for the sentencing.

Chuck Colson

"The court recognizes Mr. Colson's life of useful public service and often showing compassion for others in trouble," Judge Gesell said. Then, lifting his gavel, he said, "The court will impose a sentence of one to three years and a fine of five thousand dollars." *Whack*—the gavel fell.

Prison. Chuck felt numb. He was headed to prison.

A row of microphones, cameras, and reporters immediately surrounded Chuck and Dave as they left the courtroom. "My life is in the hands of the Lord Jesus," Chuck told them. "I can work for Christ in prison or outside it."

*   *   *

A few days before Chuck entered prison, his law partner, Charlie Morin, threw a "going-to-prison" party for him at the Palm, an exclusive Washington restaurant. About a hundred of Chuck's closest friends gathered to support him and enjoy spending one last evening with him before he began his sentence.

During one of the speeches, a little old lady came running through the crowd. At first everyone gasped—then they recognized the woman as one of Chuck's secretaries from the White House, made up with a gray wig and wire-rimmed glasses, carrying a huge purse over her shoulder. Everyone there remembered what the newspapers had said about Chuck—that he'd walk over his own grandmother if he had to. So as "Granny" ran up to Chuck, she lay down on the floor at his feet. Chuck stood glaring down at her as the photographer caught the snapshot of Colson "walking over his grandmother."

*   *   *

Four federal marshals drove Chuck through the gates of Maxwell Federal Prison Camp. The marshals led Chuck into the windowless, drab-yellow receiving building. As usual, Chuck was fingerprinted first; then they took some mug shots. Next, Colson saw the clothing officer, Mr. Blevens.

"Strip down, Colson," Blevens ordered. Every prisoner, as he entered prison, had to take off his clothes so that every item could be searched, because many prisoners tried to smuggle drugs or other forbidden things into the prison. "Can't take this," Blevens said. "Or this. Or this." Then he held up Colson's underwear. "Can't take these inside unless we don't have a pair that'll fit you." To Colson, a lawyer who was used to wearing expensive suits, this was a humiliating process.

Each of Chuck's personal items was carefully listed—including each item from Chuck's wallet, removed and listed separately. Chuck hated giving up photos of his family. Blevens also took his jewelry.

"But this class ring is like my wedding ring," Chuck said. "My wife gave this to me. Can't I keep it?"

"Rules," Blevens said. "I have to take it."

Chuck surrendered his ring—but he didn't offer to take off the chain with a small cross and dove that hung around his neck. Blevens didn't ask for it, either. He just packed all the rest of Chuck's personal things into a brown paper package to mail to Patty Colson.

Blevens tossed Colson a pair of well-worn underwear. The prison numbers of others had been written on the underwear, then crossed out. Then Blevens gave Colson his own prison number: 23226. Throughout the months of prison, this number would be more important than Chuck's name.

In his ill-fitting brown prison uniform, Chuck walked into dormitory G and found a bunk and a small locker for his few personal possessions—including a Bible. The room stank of body odor, urine, and stale tobacco smoke; dust was everywhere.

Chuck Colson

That first night, the prison guards woke Chuck every two hours as they walked through the dorm and flashed their lights in his eyes, counting the men to make sure no one escaped. Chuck slept poorly. Men were snoring, coughing, or groaning all night. Many prisoners have trouble sleeping and are liable at any hour to get up and walk around—some of them chain-smoking cigarettes.

Chuck looked forward all week to the weekend visits from Patty. They would spend both Saturday and Sunday together, sitting in the prison visiting area, talking about the events of the week. On their first weekend, Chuck was beginning to catch a cold. The brown prison uniform didn't provide much protection during the roll calls at night when the guards would count the prisoners. Patty went to her car and got an old army jacket for Chuck.

As Chuck tried on the jacket, the loudspeaker blared, "Colson! Colson! No personal possessions!" The guards had been watching Chuck and Patty. The jacket would not be allowed. Patty felt terrible. She had wanted to help her sick husband, but instead she would have to take the jacket back home.

*   *   *

During his months in prison, everything that had been important to Chuck was taken away from him: his law career, his car, his home, his family. But even prison couldn't strip away his relationship with Jesus Christ. And especially with everything else gone, this relationship with Christ became all-important to Chuck. With a few other prisoners, he began to attend a small Bible study and prayer meeting each evening. They would read the Bible and then spend time in prayer on their knees. During Chuck's months at Maxwell, this small group of men grew closer to each other and to Christ.

After several months, Chuck was transferred back to Holabird prison because Chuck's testimony was again needed at a variety of Watergate-related hearings and court cases. Patty continued visiting her husband each weekend—which was easier now that he was closer to Washington, D.C.

While Chuck was still in prison, the Virginia Supreme Court announced that he had been disbarred—which meant that he could never practice law again in that state. (He was still allowed to practice in Massachusetts.) Most of the other Watergate figures had also been disbarred, and Chuck should have expected it. But law had been a major part of his life since he was a child,

Chuck Colson

listening to his dad describe court trials as they sat on the front steps on Sunday afternoons. Now, with one legal decision, Chuck's law career was crippled.

A short time later, Colson received a phone call from his lawyer—with another piece of news that rocked Chuck even more than the disbarring.

"Chuck," his lawyer said, "your son Christian is in jail on a drug charge. He was arrested for selling drugs." Colson couldn't believe it. Chris was a college freshman who had never been in any trouble. But this time, Chuck discovered as the story unfolded, Chris had thought that he could make some quick money, so he had taken the risk—and instead he'd been caught and thrown in jail.

Because he was Colson's son, the news of Chris's arrest made national headlines and television reports. *How much more bad news can I take?* Chuck wondered.

Then one of Chuck's Christian friends from Washington called. "Chuck," Al Quie said, "there's an old, little-known law that allows a friend to serve out the rest of someone else's prison sentence during times of family difficulty. I'm going to ask the president if I can take your place."

Colson could hardly believe it. Al Quie had

served in Congress for twenty years; he was one of the most respected public figures in the country. Al Quie in prison?

"You can't be serious," Chuck said.

"Your family needs you, Chuck," Quie said.

Chuck deeply appreciated Quie's offer, but he couldn't accept it. That night as he studied his Bible, he thought about how much he was loved and supported by his brothers in Christ— and that, Chuck knew, was only a dim reflection of how much he was loved by Jesus Christ. In the quiet of his cell, Chuck prayed, "Lord, if this is what prison is all about, I praise you for leaving me here."

Two days later, Judge Gesell phoned Dave Shapiro. The judge was aware of Colson's family problems, including the drug charges against Chris. He ordered the immediate release of Colson from prison.

Dave phoned Chuck: "Pack your bags— you're leaving prison this afternoon!"

"Dave, don't fool with me. I can't take that kind of disappointment," Chuck said.

"I'm not kidding, Chuck—by the end of the day, you'll be out of there! I've got the paperwork right here."

Four hours later, Chuck Colson walked out

the doors of Holabird. After seven months in prison, he was a free man.

Sitting with Patty in the backseat of Dave Shapiro's car as they drove away, Chuck was exhausted. The months in prison and the emotional ups and downs of Watergate had taken their toll. "The days ahead will be better," Chuck promised Patty. "We'll have more time. We can travel. We won't be in the media all the time anymore."

Patty smiled and held her husband's hand—but she wasn't at all sure that he was right.

That night Chuck couldn't rest. *I've done my time in prison,* Chuck thought, lying in bed. *Now I can build a new life, find a good job, spend time with my family. I can put Watergate behind me.* But despite all that, he couldn't put prison out of his mind. He tossed and turned, drifting in and out of sleep. Suddenly he sat up in bed—he'd had a nightmare. He thought that he was back in dormitory G of Maxwell Prison; he thought that he could hear the snores and groans from men around him. As he shook himself awake, he realized that Patty was beside him. He wasn't in prison; he was at home.

Then he remembered something that had happened not long before he'd left prison. He'd been sitting and trying to read a book despite the blare of a television and the noise from the men. A big prisoner named Archie had stepped in front of him. "Hey, Colson," Archie said. "You'll be out of here before long. What are you going to do for us?"

The other men had stopped talking, wanting to hear Colson's answer.

"I'll never forget this stinking place—or you guys," Chuck promised. "I'll help you somehow."

"Yeah, that's what everybody says before they get out," Archie responded. "But nobody does anything. You'll forget us just like the rest. Nobody cares. Nobody."

"I won't forget, Archie," Chuck said. "I'll remember."

Archie's face was red with anger. "You'll forget, too, Colson! What makes you think you're any different?"

Now, lying in bed beside Patty, Chuck heard Archie's words echoing in his mind as he thought about his future—and he remembered the words of his promise: *I'll never forget this stinking place—or you guys. I'll help you somehow.*

6

Back to Prison

One Saturday morning in April after Chuck had been out of prison for a few weeks, he swung his legs out of bed and tried to convince himself to move toward the bathroom. The sun streamed through the bedroom windows of their Virginia home. Never a morning person, it usually took Chuck several cups of coffee and few slaps of cold water in the face to wake up.

Chuck dragged himself into the bathroom and began to run water into the sink to shave. He stared into the mirror at his reflection, and surprising thoughts began to come to his mind—

exciting thoughts. He could see prisoners moving in lines, dressed in their gray prison uniforms. Other thoughts came: *Prayer. Classes. Training.*

Suddenly Chuck was wide awake. "Yes—I can see it," Chuck said. "Take the prisoners out of prison, teach them, then return them to prison and form prison fellowships. It could spread across America."

With shaving cream still spread across his face, Chuck rushed to the kitchen table and pulled out his yellow legal pad. Writing quickly, he outlined a plan of action. In his mind as he wrote were the smiling faces of the prisoners who would be trained in the Good News about Christ.

Is this what the Lord wants me to do? Chuck wondered. *I'd better call Harold.* Chuck rushed back into the bathroom to wipe off the remains of the shaving cream.

Since Chuck's conversion, Harold Hughes had become used to phone calls from Chuck at all hours of the night. "Harold? Chuck. I need to see you right away. Can we get together this morning?"

Twenty minutes later, Harold sat in Chuck's basement office, sipping coffee. With excitement, Chuck explained his plan to take prison-

Chuck Colson

ers all across America out of prison temporarily for training.

Harold listened carefully and then said, "It's of God. No doubt." Then he frowned. "But there are hundreds of prisons. How could we even begin? It's impossible."

"Not with God. 'All things are possible,'" Chuck quoted from the words of Jesus.

During his years as governor of Iowa, Hughes had tried to start some programs of prison reform, but he hadn't been successful. Because of that experience, he knew how difficult Chuck's vision would be to bring to reality.

The two men spent the morning praying and talking together. "It should all get started with a visit to Senator Eastland," Harold suggested near the end of their meeting. Senator James Eastland was the chairman of the powerful Senate Judiciary Committee, which handled all laws related to the prisons and criminal matters.

Senator Hughes used his friendship with Eastland to set up a meeting. Two weeks later, Hughes and Colson walked into Senator Eastland's large office.

The southern senator held an unlighted cigar as they sat and talked. Chuck described the problems and horrors of prison life. After a few minutes, Senator Eastland leaned forward and said, peering through his wire-rimmed glasses, "Maxwell. You didn't mind it, did you? That's a nice place."

"Have you ever been there, Senator?"

"I've got a lot of people from my state there," he said with a chuckle. "But no. I've never been there."

"Have you ever been to a prison, Senator?" Chuck asked.

"No—this job keeps me pretty busy," the senator replied.

For almost two hours Colson and Hughes talked with Senator Eastland. In the end, the senator promised to look into the possibilities of Chuck's plan.

But as the weeks passed, neither Senator Hughes or Colson heard anything more from Senator Eastland. The idea of prison reform was quietly buried in the papers on Senator Eastland's desk. The two men talked with several other officials, but no one seemed interested.

Every Monday, Chuck attended a regular meeting for prayer and fellowship. At one of those meetings, Chuck asked Harold, "What if we went right to the head of the Bureau of Prisons?"

Chuck Colson

"Couldn't hurt," Harold said. "Who's the director?"

"Norman Carlson. Let's try a very straight-forward approach—let's tell him that we want to meet and talk about how to bring Jesus Christ into the prisons." Their unusual approach worked. Hughes and Colson had an appointment for the next day.

*   *   *

It was a sunny June morning, and Hughes, Colson, and Fred Rhodes stopped in front of the old Bureau of Prisons building just a few blocks from the Capitol building. They prayed briefly that God would touch Norman Carlson's heart and open the doors for a ministry to the prisons.

Carlson greeted them with a smile and led them into his inner office, a comfortable and attractive room furnished with orange sofas. "By the way, I was born in Iowa," Carlson volunteered. Since Senator Hughes represented Iowa, the two of them spent several minutes discussing matters of interest to that state. Then, with Carlson's permission, Senator Hughes opened their meeting with a short prayer.

"Mr. Carlson," Senator Hughes began, "we're here today to tell you about a new idea for the federal prisons. Chuck will tell you about it."

Then, as he had with Senator Eastland, Chuck told about his own prison experience and his relationship with Jesus Christ. He described the problems of the prison system—such as the fact that in most states, eighty percent of the prisoners return to prison after their release because they had committed additional crimes. This, of course, was a dangerous argument to present to a man who had spent his life running the prisons of the United States. But Carlson, rather than becoming offended and defensive, listened with interest.

"Mr. Carlson, the prisons aren't helping. Only one person can make a difference. That's Jesus Christ. Give us a chance to prove it." Chuck went on to outline his plan to take prisoners out of the federal prisons for training.

"Is that it?" Carlson asked.

"Yes, sir."

"Well, I'm not denying that there's a lot of truth in what you say about prisons. Let me ask you a question." Then Carlson told about a recent visit to Terminal Island Prison in Southern California. Carlson and his wife had attended a chapel service there, and during the service, they heard a prisoner praying for them. As a prison-system official, Carlson had been surprised by the prayer. He had thought that he'd be

Chuck Colson

the last person prisoners would pray for. "Why did he do that?" Carlson asked.

"I'm not surprised. That man is a Christian, and we're told in the Bible to pray for our leaders," Chuck said. "When I was in prison, I prayed for the warden."

"But I'm keeping that man in prison," Carlson objected.

"Mr. Carlson, that man prayed for you because he loves you."

It was a powerful moment. Carlson shook his head, unsure what to make of all this. But as Colson and Hughes walked out of the office at the end of the meeting, Carlson said, "Gentlemen—go ahead with your plans. I'll issue the order. Just get together with my staff to work out the details."

The two men walked out of that aging government building feeling as if their feet weren't touching the ground. The door for ministry to America's prisons had been opened—partly because of the prayer of one unknown prisoner for the head of the U.S. prison system.

*   *   *

After his release from prison, Chuck wrote a book about his experiences in the White House and his newfound relationship with Christ. *Born*

Again was published in 1976. It immediately became popular.

Chuck began to receive speaking invitations from all over the U.S. People wanted to hear for themselves about Chuck's new faith in Christ. Chuck saw each of these meetings as a chance to talk about the spiritual needs of prisoners.

Chuck was not the only person from Nixon's White House staff who went to prison as a result of Watergate; in fact, there were several. Some of the others, after their release from prison, accepted good-paying job offers—but not Chuck Colson. He received the same type of offers but refused to take them. One chief executive of a large company in Dallas said to Colson, "I can make you a millionaire within five years."

Chuck considered the offer and then told the executive, "No—I've been called into the prisons."

During the summer of 1976, Chuck and Patty made a trip to the West Coast. "Chuck, whatever you decide about your future, I'll support you," Patty told him during that trip. By the time they returned to Washington, a friend, Fred Rhodes, had drafted official legal documents to begin a prison ministry. Some people wanted to include Chuck's name in the organization name, but Chuck said, "No, the name should focus on our goal—prison ministry."

Chuck used about seventy-five thousand dollars from his first royalty check from *Born Again* to start Prison Fellowship. He rented a small office for three hundred dollars a month. The office was so empty that some of the six-person staff didn't even have chairs and had to sit on the floor! Chuck's son, Wendell, made some homemade furniture from fiberboard to furnish the Prison Fellowship office. Chuck donated all of his speaking fees and much of the earnings from his books to the ministry of Prison Fellowship. Even though he was its founder, Chuck decided not to receive a salary from Prison Fellowship for its first several years.

Instead of using his vast experience to increase his own wealth and power through business, Chuck had chosen to start a ministry to some of the least powerful people in the world—people whom, even though they'd been forgotten by nearly everyone else, he could not forget.

*   *   *

As the sun crept over the city of Washington, another day was starting. Chuck had been up for hours—he was headed for the airport to begin another trip, visiting prisons and speaking at churches and banquets. Usually, Chuck traveled with his executive assistant, Mike Cromartie, a young, single man responsible for Chuck's schedule. But on this trip, Mike wasn't coming.

"Why don't you take some time off, Mike?" Chuck had suggested. "Fred Rhodes can go with me on this trip, and you can stay home." Mike agreed to take a much-needed break from traveling. And since he didn't have to pack for another early-morning trip, Mike planned to sleep late.

Chuck picked up Fred Rhodes at his house that morning and said with a grin, "Let's go by and see if Mike's up."

Fred looked at his watch. "It's five-thirty!" It was unlikely that Mike would even be awake, much less out of bed.

When they arrived at Mike's house, Chuck walked onto his porch and tried the door. Finding it unlocked, Chuck walked right into the house. Stumbling around because he'd never been inside Mike's house before, Chuck went into the first bedroom he came to—and found Mike's roommate, still sound asleep. "Where's Mike?" Chuck asked.

Chuck Colson

"Mike's in the other room," the roommate mumbled and then turned over.

Chuck barged into the next bedroom and hollered, "Mike, we're ready to go! Where's your suit bag?"

Hearing the voice of his boss, Mike jumped out of bed and gave Chuck a salute. "Yes, sir! I'll be ready in a minute." Mike hurriedly began looking around for his suitcase—and then suddenly remembered. "Hey—Fred's going on this trip. I'm staying ho—"

Chuck laughed and then waved good-bye. He was off to the airport. The expression on Mike's face had made it worth losing an extra half-hour of sleep.

Chuck's life was hectic, but jokes like that one gave it some welcome comic relief.

*   *   *

"Ralston won't let us take prisoners out," Prison Fellowship staffer Paul Kramer told Chuck. Warden George Ralston was in charge of the Federal Correctional Institution in Oxford, Wisconsin. In most prisons, Prison Fellowship operated by taking small groups of prisoners outside of prison, training them in the Bible, and then returning them. But this warden wouldn't budge. Instead of releasing the prisoners,

Ralston suggested that the seminar be held inside the prison.

So Chuck and several others in the Prison Fellowship office planned a seminar to be held inside the prison. Then they recruited twenty-five Wisconsin Christians to join them in presenting the seminar. Ninety-five prisoners attended the three days of teaching—among them, ten Black Muslims who sat together at one table.

On the last day of the seminar, Warden Ralston asked to meet with Chuck in his office. "What a tremendous week!" the warden said, delighted and amazed. "You should do this in *every* prison. And I'll be happy to recommend it."

Chuck thanked the warden and said, "You made it possible."

"Nonsense," Ralston said. "It's my duty to see that these men have an opportunity to better themselves. You've got something to offer that will help them to do that, and I intend to take advantage of it."

Because of this warden's challenge, Colson and the staff of Prison Fellowship began a new type of ministry—seminars held inside the prisons. It would prove to be a great idea: Within ten years, Prison Fellowship would be holding as many as three hundred-fifty in-prison seminars a year, and within twenty years, over *two thousand* a year.

Besides Chuck's speaking and appearances in prisons, Prison Fellowship organized volunteers to hold Bible studies and share the Good News about Christ in prisons. After only four years, Prison Fellowship was operating in the U.S., Australia, Canada, and England. With an annual budget of two million dollars, they coordinated the activities of six thousand volunteers.

*   *   *

The public remembered Chuck from his Watergate days. Even though several years had passed since Chuck had been making daily headlines, sometimes strong feelings surfaced in unusual ways. In San Francisco, Chuck spoke to the Young Presidents' Association. After the speech, as Chuck and Mike headed toward the elevator, a young reporter from the *Berkeley Barb*, a radical newspaper, stopped for a brief interview. "Don't let that guy interview you—those people hate us," one of the leaders murmured to Chuck.

"That's the kind of people we want to talk to. We've got nothing to hide," Mike said as he led Chuck over to the reporter.

The *Berkeley Barb* reporter asked several

hostile questions, which Chuck answered as well as he could. Finally Chuck excused himself, saying, "We've got to go now. We've got to get to the airport." As they waited for the elevator to arrive, they stood in front of the elevator doors talking with some of the association leaders.

The elevator arrived. Mike and Chuck stepped inside and the door began to close. Just then the reporter yelled, "Mr. Colson! Mr. Colson! Just one more question!" Mike punched the open-door button on the elevator control panel—watching in amazement as the reporter flipped a chocolate-cream pie right in Chuck's face. Chocolate pie dripped off Chuck's suit as Mike ran through the fancy hotel lobby and tackled the reporter. "Don't hurt me," the man pleaded, held firmly down by Colson's tall, lanky assistant.

"Just let him go," Chuck said. "We don't want to get back at him. Let's go up to our rooms."

Shortly after Chuck and Mike left, the *Berkeley Barb* reporter held a press conference of his own. "I've always wanted to be able to tell my grandchildren I threw a pie in the face of someone from Watergate," he said into the microphones.

The news about Colson's getting a pie in the

Chuck Colson

face spread quickly across the national news-papers, radio, and television. In fact, while Chuck and Mike were still in the air on their way from San Francisco to Los Angeles, Patty Colson, driving her car on the other side of the country, heard about the pie-throwing incident on her car radio.

From the hotel in Los Angeles, Chuck called his wife. "You'll never guess what happened to me," he said. "Well, let me guess—you got hit in the face with a pie."

"How did you know?" Chuck asked with surprise.

"I heard it on my car radio," Patty said.

*   *   *

During those early years of Prison Fellowship, Chuck faced a lot of skepticism from people who had a hard time believing that Chuck Colson, Nixon's "Hatchet Man," had a genuine spiritual relationship with Jesus Christ. Chuck had to not only endure the criticism and doubts of these skeptics but also to win them over. And the skeptics weren't always in the pul-pits or offices—sometimes they were behind bars.

In Walla Walla, Washington, the large prison is located in a remote area outside the town.

"We're going to take you into the sex-offender unit," the prison chaplain explained. Sex-offender units are often isolated from the other sections of the prison because most prisoners don't like the men who have committed these violent crimes against women and children.

About one hundred men lived in a single room. There were six people in Chuck's party, with Mike Cromartie leading the group. Mike walked into that room first, saw the roughest-looking bunch of men he had ever seen—and immediately made a U-turn and walked out. "I'll follow you," he said to Chuck.

Wearing a blue sport coat and a red tie, Chuck walked into the meeting room. The men stared at Colson skeptically. Most of them knew that Chuck Colson had worked for the president of the United States. After the chaplain's brief introduction, Chuck began to speak: "I know what it's like to be here. You've heard of Watergate—I made mistakes, and I had to pay for them. I've been here, too. Now I work with a ministry called Prison Fellowship. Let me tell you how that happened." Then Chuck would tell how he came to believe in Jesus Christ.

The men listened. Some continued to stare hostilely, their arms folded across their chests. But others were touched—and their resistance melted as God spoke to them, using Chuck's sincere words.

That experience was repeated in prison after prison, as, slowly, word spread—*Colson is real. Colson cares about what's happening to us in prison. Colson is our friend.*

*   *   *

It was not the only tense experience at the prison in Walla Walla for Chuck and his team. One crisp morning in October 1979, surrounded by gentle green hills just beginning to turn orange and brown, Chuck stepped out of his car and stared at the prison. "Concrete Mama," as it was called by prisoners, was considered by many to be one of the toughest institutions in the U.S. When the American Corrections Association inspected Walla Walla Prison, they said it was one of the worst—overcrowded, dirty, and out of control. The prison even had an inmate biker group that roughed up the guards and other inmates.

Four months before Chuck's visit, a guard had been killed, and the prison had been locked down ever since—meaning that the prisoners had to stay in their cells for the entire day except for one hour. Fifty-eight guards had staged a strike during the lockdown, and most of them had been fired and replaced.

"When were the men released from the lockdown?" Chuck asked a guard as he stepped up to the prison gate.

"Yesterday. But don't worry. Riot police are standing by."

Some comfort, Chuck thought, *in one of America's toughest prisons. Which one of my staff set up this speaking date?*

The assistant warden, a former priest, waved and stuck out his hand. "Mr. Colson, I'm glad you're here."

"What's it feel like inside?" Chuck asked.

"Tense, I suppose," the man said with a shrug. "I don't get into the population much. I'm sure whatever you can do will help."

As Colson and the others from Prison Fellowship toured the cellblocks and the prison yard, they discovered that the descriptions of the prison hadn't been exaggerated; it was incredibly overcrowded and dirty.

Tension hung in the air, and it didn't take the Fellowship staff long to figure out why. Most of the prisoners were angry about their prison yard. Before the lockdown, the only green grass inside the prison walls had been a small athletic field in the center of the prison, but during the four-month lockdown, even that small area of grass had been covered with tons of concrete. Prison officials said they had done it for security reasons, but the lack of grass seemed to be making the prisoners more angry and increasing the risk of violence.

At 2:00 P.M., Senior Chaplain Jerry Jacobson escorted Chuck into a large auditorium that seated a thousand men. But when the chaplain introduced Colson, there were eight hundred-fifty empty chairs and one hundred-fifty unresponsive inmates.

Chuck started his talk by telling the stories of the beginning days of Prison Fellowship. But even stories that almost always got a laugh today got only stone cold silence.

Chuck noticed, on the front row, two older inmates sitting straight, arms folded. As he delivered the final words of his talk, Colson concentrated on them.

Well, at least there wasn't any trouble, Chuck told himself afterward, walking across the prison yard. Just then a gruff voice called out his name. Turning, Chuck spotted the two older prisoners from the front row. One of them, a man who looked to be in his late forties, with graying hair, stuck out his hand and said, "I'm Don

Dennis. We've been talking about you, and we believe you."

"Yeah," the other man nodded, slapping Colson's back.

"I can't tell you how glad I am to hear that. We'll do everything we can to help you," Chuck promised.

A few days later, Chuck asked George Soltau, an experienced Prison Fellowship instructor, to teach two Bible study seminars at Walla Walla Prison. George could tell, as soon as he arrived, that tensions were still high. He met privately with the prisoner Don Dennis—and learned, to his amazement, what far-reaching effects had sprung from Chuck's message.

After Colson's talk in that nearly empty auditorium, the leaders of the prisoners had called off a riot. The prisoners had been planning to murder six guards. When they had heard that Chuck Colson would be visiting the prison about the time of their planned riot, some of the prisoners had talked about taking Colson as a hostage. But after they heard him speak, the prisoners decided that they could trust Colson and that they would ask for his help instead. As George listened to Don Dennis, he decided that they needed Chuck's help. He discovered, for instance, that for eighteen months there had been no meaningful communication between prison officials and prisoners.

In the months that followed, George Soltau and others from Prison Fellowship worked to help prison officials and the prisoners in Walla Walla begin to talk with each other. Progress was slow at times, but at least the tension eased and there was no riot.

On the Prison Fellowship stationery, they include a Bible verse from the prophet Isaiah, "A bruised reed he will not break. . . . In faithfulness he will bring forth justice" (Isaiah 42:3). Chuck, George, and the others in Prison Fellowship had taken God at his word, and their experience in Walla Walla Prison showed that his Word could be trusted.

7

A Place
of Great Need

Not every door in the prison system automatically opened to Chuck Colson and Prison Fellowship. Sometimes trust had to be earned first. There were some chaplains, for instance, who wondered about Colson. Would he throw his political weight around and replace them? Would he try to undermine the ministry they had already worked hard to establish? During those early years, Chuck worked hard to reassure the chaplains. Prison Fellowship wanted to work *alongside* these men and women, to help their ministry—not to replace them.

During a trip to Atlanta, Chuck met Tim Ondahl, affectionately known at the Atlanta Prison as the "hippie priest." At first, this tall, bearded man regarded Colson with some skepticism. Did Colson have a real commitment to Christ? Father Ondahl knew that there were lots of fakers—and he also knew that fakers were easily exposed in the harsh atmosphere of prison. In the past sixteen months, there had been more than ten brutal murders at the Atlanta Prison. Prison officials had clamped down on the two thousand prisoners, but the fear level among the inmates was still high.

Throughout that week before Colson's visit to the Atlanta Prison, Prison Fellowship had held an in-prison seminar to teach inmates how to grow in their faith in Jesus Christ. One afternoon, Colson, the prison chaplain Charlie Riggs, Father Ondahl, and several others came to the prison. Paul Kramer, from Prison Fellowship, greeted the party. "Chuck, the seminar's going great—but things are really tense inside."

For the first time since the clampdown, the warden had opened the meeting to the entire prison population. Before the session began, Chuck and the others met with a few prisoners.

One told Chuck that many of the men would be surprised that Chuck had even shown up at the meeting. Apparently, the warden had been saying good things about Chuck—and that had made the men suspicious. After all, if the warden likes him, why should the prisoners? To make matters worse, the heat was sweltering and the humidity high.

"And by the way," one of the men told Chuck, "no preaching about Jesus."

Chuck protested. "That's why I *came* to Atlanta—to preach the Good News about Jesus."

"Maybe you could talk about prison reform instead," someone suggested.

Heads nodded in agreement. That would be a safe topic.

Reluctantly Chuck agreed. After prayer, the men walked into the meeting place where over eight hundred prisoners waited.

Tension hung in the air as the service began. Father Ondahl gave the opening prayer. By this time, though, Father Ondahl's opinion of Chuck Colson had changed. He had spent a few hours with him, and discovered that this man really cared about prisoners. "We're a mixed bag, Father," the priest prayed. "We're happy to know that your message fits us all. Help us to believe, but even more, help us to practice the teachings of your Son, our Brother, Jesus Christ. Amen."

When Chuck stood up to speak, he looked out over the crowd and saw their stern expressions—even the ones he knew. "You may wonder why we're here," he said. Many of the prisoners nodded. "You've heard that I was in the White House. You've also heard that I committed crimes and went to prison. I've been where you are . . ."

Chuck described the early days of Prison Fellowship. He told how Christ had changed his life and the lives of many prisoners. Except for Chuck's voice, the room was dead silent.

"Jesus came for you and he came for me. Jesus came to the hurting people to set them free," Chuck said. When he had finished, he said a simple prayer. As he sat down, the men rose to their feet, clapping. The faces that had been stern and unsmiling were smiling now, and tears glistened on the cheeks of those hardened prisoners. Afterward, Chuck stood for over an hour, talking with one inmate after another.

One well-known member of the mafia, a man called Joe the Butcher, prayed with Chuck, asking Jesus to forgive his sins and change his life. A number of Joe's buddies also prayed that day.

Chuck Colson

As Chuck walked outside the prison, he knew that he had understood God correctly on that morning many years before, sitting at the kitchen table with shaving cream on his face. Prison ministry was indeed his calling. And the experience of that meeting he had just come out of illustrated as well as anything why he worked in prisons. In these dark, forgotten holes, Chuck experienced a deep fellowship with men who were much like the people Jesus had taught and healed when he walked the earth.

* * *

The sun hadn't yet crept over the horizon on this Easter morning in 1982. For the fourth straight year, Chuck and a group from Prison Fellowship planned to hold a sunrise service in a prison on Easter morning. This year, it would be at Indiana State Penitentiary in Terre Haute, and the group numbered about twenty, including several local volunteers Chuck hadn't met before.

Prisons are the tombs of our world, Chuck thought. *This must be what Jesus would want us to do—visit those in prison so we can celebrate together the risen Jesus.*

Colson's group, which included recording artist Nancy Honeytree carrying her guitar, passed through the security checks, walked through the double-locked gates, and crossed a walled courtyard surrounded by tall, gray guard towers.

They entered the small auditorium and greeted the men who were gathered for the Easter service. Chuck opened his Bible and began: "The world outside is looking for Easter bunnies laying pink and purple eggs," he said. "But if Christ were on earth today, where would he be? In the rotten, stinking joints of this world, preaching the Gospel to the poor and proclaiming the release of the captives."

When the service was over, Chuck told Superintendent Duckworth, "I'd like to go to death row. You just had an execution of one of the inmates there, and the others may need someone to talk to about it. In fact, I've been corresponding with two of the men there."

The group from Prison Fellowship wound through the prison, passing through several internal gates and checkpoints. Finally they reached the sealed area of the prison called death row. In these cells, ten men sentenced to execution—some of them still teenagers—were isolated from the rest of the prisoners.

Colson and the rest walked past the thick steel bars of the cells. Most of the cells were dark. Some prisoners rolled over in bed to look at Chuck and the others as they walked past. Many of the cells were decorated with obscene calendars and photos.

The group climbed a set of metal steps to a catwalk on the second floor, where they clunked past another set of darkened cells. As they approached the end of the hallway, they could see one cell ahead from which light spilled out. When they reached it, they found that, instead of pornographic photos, this cell was decorated with words—words from the Bible. Richard Moore, who had come to Christ through volunteers in Prison Fellowship, was already awake and praying in his cell. Suddenly the atmosphere changed. Even on death row, here was a group of believers sharing their excitement and joy about the risen Christ on Easter morning.

Honeytree sang a few songs. Richard Moore held his Bible high as the group sang together, "He Lives."

"Chuck, I knew you would come," Richard said when the singing was over. "As soon as I heard you were coming to the prison, I knew you'd stop by my cell to encourage me."

The other Christian man Chuck had come to death row to see was James Brewer, a young black man. While waiting for his death sentence,

Chuck Colson

James had grown seriously ill from a kidney disease. Even so, he had maintained a powerful witness about Jesus Christ to others on death row.

After Chuck's visit with Brewer, the Prison Fellowship group sang, "Amazing Grace" and Chuck began moving everyone toward the exit. He was growing anxious about the time. At a nearby airstrip, a plane waited to fly Chuck into Indianapolis, where he would see the Indiana governor. As he was about to shepherd everyone through the exit, he noticed one of the local volunteers still standing by the cell of James Brewer.

With one more glance at his watch—it was getting late—Chuck walked over and said to the short white man standing close to the bars of Brewer's cell, an open Bible in his hand, "I'm sorry, but we have to leave."

The man looked up at Chuck, "Just give us another minute, please. This is important."

His patience running thin after the long, tiring day, Chuck snapped, "No, I'm sorry, but I can't keep the governor waiting. We must go."

The man responded softly, "I understand— but this is important. You see, I'm Judge Clement. I sentenced James Brewer to die. Now James is my brother, and we want a minute to pray together."

Chuck stepped back, shocked and awed by what was happening before him. Suddenly, it didn't matter whom he kept waiting. Here were two men, one with power and one powerless. One had sentenced the other to death. If they weren't brothers in Christ, Brewer might have wanted to kill the judge for his sentence. Now, instead, they were praying together in love and joy.

Later the judge told Chuck, "Since I sentenced Brewer four years ago, I've been praying for him every day."

As they walked out of the Indiana Penitentiary, his upcoming meeting with the governor seemed far less important than what he had just seen. Once again, firsthand, Chuck had watched the power of Christ tear down barriers and build a sense of love and caring between people who might otherwise have been filled with hate and bitterness. *This is the real power, the power of Christ to change lives,* Chuck thought. *Compared to this, the power I had in the White House is nothing.*

* * *

Prison Fellowship continued to grow and to create other ways to touch the lives of prisoners. In 1982, Prison Fellowship started a program called Angel Tree. The families of those in

Chuck Colson

prison often don't have much of a Christmas celebration. Why not enlist volunteers from local churches to provide some Christmas cheer and presents for those families? In Angel Tree's first year, Prison Fellowship gave churches the names and ages of children of prisoners in their area. Volunteers from those churches bought toys and clothing, wrapped them, and delivered them to over five hundred-fifty children. Only three years later, the program was helping twenty thousand children. Ten years later, it reached over two hundred-sixty thousand children with gifts during the Christmas season.

By 1985, Prison Fellowship International had expanded to work in twenty-eight countries around the world. The staff in Washington and Virginia had spread out into three different office locations. In 1987, only ten years after the beginning of the ministry, the two hundred staff members moved into a new Prison Fellowship office building in Reston, Virginia. They coordinated the efforts of more than twenty-five thousand volunteers.

*   *   *

Chuck still considered himself to be relatively young in his faith in Jesus Christ. To learn and grow, he read many books and met every chance he got with Christian leaders. And from each pastor or teacher he met, Chuck learned more about how to follow Jesus.

The Reverend Neal Jones was one of these men from whom Chuck learned. When Chuck and Patty were at the Prison Fellowship headquarters in Washington, they attended the church where Jones was the pastor—Columbia Baptist Church. One day Chuck came to visit the Reverend Jones in his study.

"If you want to keep growing, Chuck, you need to establish a regular time with the Lord," the Reverend Jones explained. Then he helped Chuck set a time for Bible reading and a time for prayer.

Like a dry sponge, Chuck drank in teaching from any source. "Trying to teach Chuck is like nailing Jello to a wall," the Reverend Jones says. "He absorbs so rapidly and then moves on to the next point."

Other men who spent time teaching Chuck about Jesus Christ during those early days included R. C. Sproul of Ligonier Ministries, Richard Lovelace of Gordon-Conwell Seminary, and the theologian Carl Henry.

Jim Jewell eventually replaced Mike Cromartie as Chuck's traveling companion and associate. During one of their flights, Jim used the restroom on the airplane—but when he tried to exit, Jim couldn't get the restroom door open. He pulled, pushed, twisted, and tugged on the handle, but it wouldn't budge.

As much as he could in such a confined space, Jim leaned back to take a flying lunge at the door. He gathered his strength, rushed at the door—and it gave way easily and flew open. Jim sprawled across the aisle of the airplane.

Out of the corner of his eye, Jim saw Chuck scurrying back down the aisle of the plane toward his seat. It didn't take Jim long to figure out why his bathroom door had been "stuck."

*   *   *

As Chuck well remembers from his own days in prison, holidays are difficult times for prisoners. That's why, besides his Easter visits, Chuck sometimes makes Christmas visits, too. On Christmas Day in 1985, Chuck was speaking at a women's prison in North Carolina. After the service, a prison official asked Chuck, "Would you like to visit Bessie Shipp? She's in solitary."

"Of course," Chuck answered. He visited the death row and solitary-confinement areas of prisons every chance he got. Those areas gave him a great chance to share Christ with prisoners one-on-one.

"One thing you should know," the official added. "Bessie has AIDS."

In 1985, the deadly disease, AIDS, had just broken out, and little was known about it; there was a lot of uncertainty about how it could be transmitted from person to person. Would Chuck risk getting AIDS by seeing this prisoner?

Then he remembered seeing a story on last night's news about Mother Teresa's work at an AIDS hospice. Chuck had watched as Mother Teresa, the Catholic nun, gently held dying patients in New York City. "They need to know God loves them," she had said.

And so on that Christmas morning in 1985, Chuck entered the cell where Bessie Shipp lay alone and dying. He took Bessie's hand—it felt cold. As simply as he could, he told Bessie about the most important decision she would ever make—to accept Jesus Christ as her personal Savior.

Bessie listened and prayed with Chuck. She received Christ as her Savior. Three weeks later, Bessie Shipp left that cold, lonely cell and entered the presence of the Lord Jesus.

Few people have ever heard of Bessie Shipp. In the eyes of the world, she was just

Chuck Colson

another prisoner, just another AIDS victim, just someone who died alone and was forgotten years ago. But she was someone Jesus loved enough to die for. And meeting her was, for Chuck Colson, a life-changing experience.

"Prison Fellowship is not just some vague group for prisons," Chuck wrote later. "We are dealing with life and death. We'd better get on with this business of proclaiming the Gospel of Jesus!" Meeting Bessie, hearing her pray, had given Chuck a fresh sense of urgency for telling others about Christ—before they died.

Another holiday, another year: Easter 1990.

Chuck and a few people from Prison Fellowship went to the old Central Correctional Institution near the river in downtown Columbia, South Carolina. As the world celebrated the empty tomb of Jesus, Chuck and his staff entered this maximum-security prison to celebrate with Christian prisoners. For these prisoners in South Carolina, on this year, Easter held a special significance: It came just eleven days before the execution of convicted murderer Rusty Woomer.

Although Rusty would soon be strapped into an electric chair for his execution, he faced death with tears of joy. "When I think about God's love and radiance and power," Rusty told that group of Christians that day after reading aloud some of his poetry, "doesn't it scare you that someone loves you enough that he can forgive you for anything that you do?"

*　　*　　*

Patty Colson opened the door to the Colsons' Virginia apartment. Ellen Vaughn, senior writer for Prison Fellowship, stood in the entryway. "Come in, Ellen—Chuck's been expecting you."

Chuck and Ellen had written a number of books together, but lately, Chuck's demanding schedule had been on hold. Doctors had discovered a growth in his stomach. To surgically remove the growth, they also had to remove part of his stomach, and his recovery had been slow.

Now the two of them sat in Chuck's living room, working on a new book; Chuck still wore his brown-striped pajamas. Their deadline was approaching, and Chuck was determined to finish on schedule.

Chuck was trying to drink a milk shake as they discussed some of the pages of the book, but his stomach wasn't handling it very well.

Ellen looked up from the pages and noticed flecks of foam around Chuck's mouth as he talked. "Chuck, are you okay? Want to do this some other time?" Ellen suggested. "If you aren't well, we can do it later."

Chuck shook his head. He felt pretty rotten, actually—but once Chuck committed himself to a goal, he had a hard time letting it slide. Chuck was driven by his goals—he hated to fail to accomplish what he set out to do. "No—we have a deadline," Chuck said, "and if we're going to meet it, we've got to finish this." By the end of their work session, Ellen and Chuck had met their goal for that particular day.

*   *   *

Each year, Prison Fellowship holds hundreds of in-prison seminars to teach prisoners how to grow and share their faith in Jesus. In 1991, the five thousandth seminar was held. Life Plan Seminars, where inmates are taught how to set goals, manage money, and find employment and friends, are another Prison Fellowship program. And there are currently about nine hundred active Bible study groups in prisons led by Prison Fellowship volunteers. These are just a few of the programs that Chuck Colson and his staff have launched to reach into prisons around the world.

It was into one of those prisons in California that Chuck and several of his associates from

Prison Fellowship walked one day a few years ago. Only minutes before they arrived, the warden had locked down the prisoners, taking away what few freedoms they possessed. His reason for the lockdown was that the leaders of two gangs had decided to fight it out for control of the prison. Because these gang leaders were planning to use the Prison Fellowship gathering as a way to reach each other, the warden canceled all meetings—including the Prison Fellowship session.

The prison chaplain, disappointed and concerned that the prisoners would not be able to hear Chuck and the others from Prison Fellowship, pulled some men together to pray about it. Afterward, the chaplain pleaded with the warden for the event to continue. Reluctantly, the warden agreed—the meeting could take place.

A restless group of prisoners gathered in rows to hear Chuck Colson speak. Members of the two gangs, wearing their distinctive tattoos, were scattered throughout the crowd. The warden's worst fears were about to be realized—the gangs intended to go ahead with their original plan and disrupt the meeting with violence. "I'm going to get Colson," one gang member mumbled to the prisoner sitting next to him.

When Chuck stood up to speak, he noticed a group of eight or nine gang members watching him carefully from the back of the crowd. Establishing eye contact with them, he began to tell his story—first about his time in prison, and then about the love Christ had given him for prisoners. Chuck spoke with energy and with power, and the prisoners, despite their intentions to disrupt the meeting, listened carefully. As he finished his talk, Chuck said, "I'm going to give you an opportunity to make a decision that can change your life—to accept Jesus Christ. You can pray this prayer with me tonight: 'Lord Jesus, I'm a sinner. I need you. Come into my life right now. Thank you for forgiving me of my sins. In Jesus' name, amen.' Then Chuck looked out across the crowd. "If you prayed that prayer with me, raise your hand and let me know it," he said.

Four of the gang members in the back of the room raised their hands.

After the meeting, one of the gang members who had not raised his hand—one of the toughest of them—said, "I don't know what was happening during that meeting, but something sure was. I decided not to disturb it. It wasn't the right thing to do."

Later in the day, the prison chaplain led several of the rival gang leaders to Christ. Lives had been changed; the spiritual life of many prisoners had been changed forever—and once again, it had started with a simple visit from Chuck Colson and his Prison Fellowship associates, in quiet obedience to Jesus Christ.

By 1991, Prison Fellowship had grown to a paid staff of three hundred-ten working in forty-eight states and forty countries. They had mobilized forty thousand volunteers. Each day, thousands of prisoners were being touched for Christ.

8

Chuck Gives Away a Million Dollars

"**W**hat can you tell me about this Reverend Wilbert Forker who's coming to see me?" Chuck asked Tom Pratt, the Chief Executive Officer of Prison Fellowship, over the phone.

"The Reverend Forker is the executive vice-president for the Templeton Foundation," Tom explained.

Chuck already knew about the Templeton Foundation, established by Sir John Templeton.

He knew that, each year, the foundation awards the Templeton Prize for Progress in Religion to some person or ministry. The award is 650,000 British pounds sterling—over a million dollars—which makes it the world's largest annual prize. Other recipients of this prize have included Billy Graham and Mother Teresa.

What Chuck didn't know was that his staff at Prison Fellowship had been working behind the scenes to nominate him to receive the award. He found that out when the Reverend Forker arrived—and informed Chuck that he had been selected as the 1993 winner of the Templeton Prize.

To say that Chuck was amazed when he found out that he had won the award is an understatement. The truth was, Chuck felt traumatized. But after he'd gotten over his initial shock, he felt grateful to God. It had been seventeen years since Chuck had left prison. Prison Fellowship, the ministry he had founded, now coordinated the activities of over fifty thousand people around the world who had volunteered to work in the prisons. The ministry had now spread to fifty-four countries and had an annual budget of over twenty million dollars. Chuck knew that none of that had been accomplished through his own power but rather, through the grace of God, and Chuck felt grateful that God had allowed him to be a part of it.

"Make out the check to Prison Fellowship," Chuck told the Revered Forker. "I won't keep any that money for myself."

Patty Colson agreed. "That money is not ours but God's," she said.

*   *   *

At a ceremony at the United Nations building in New York, where the Templeton Prize winner was officially announced, Chuck said, "When I first learned of this award, I did not feel a sense of exultation. I was instead driven to my knees, humbled and grateful to the Lord Jesus Christ whom I serve. . . . By God's grace, he has chosen to take a person from the shame and disgrace of Watergate and prison and use him to build a prison movement in fifty-four countries. The funds will be used to further strengthen that work, particularly among prisoners' families. I am humbled. To God be the glory."

In May 1993, Chuck and Patty Colson and Chuck's two adult sons, Christian and Wendell, boarded an airplane for London, England. Each year the actual Templeton Prize was given by Prince Philip in a private ceremony in Buckingham Palace. The Queen of England can't give the award because she is the head of the Church of England.

But Chuck didn't spend his entire trip hobnobbing with royalty. On the day of the presentation, he passed first through the stone walls of Pentonville Prison, outside London. He had an opportunity to share the Good News about Jesus with the prisoners there, and that's not the kind of opportunity Chuck was likely to pass up.

Later, Chuck, Patty, and his two sons went to Buckingham Palace. The small group, which included Sir John Templeton, was ushered into a back entrance of the Palace. They climbed a set of stairs and entered an ornate room decorated in Chinese style.

Several aides of Prince Philip gave the party some instructions before the prince arrived. "Don't speak unless spoken to, and never bring up a subject unless the prince introduces it," one said.

When Prince Philip arrived, he greeted each member of the Templeton party. In a simple ceremony, the prince gave Chuck the check with the prize money and a medal inscribed with his name.

"What you think should be done about prison reform, Mr. Colson?" the prince asked. Chuck launched into a fifteen-minute speech

Chuck Colson

about prison reform. The prince seemed genuinely interested in what Chuck had to say.

"It's only because Jesus Christ has changed my life that I can be here accepting this award for Prison Fellowship," Chuck concluded, and then explained briefly about Prison Fellowship and its worldwide ministry in prisons.

After meeting with the prince for half an hour, the group left the palace. Chuck turned to the others and said, "I'm glad that today I got to go from prison to the palace—it's sure a lot better than twenty years ago when I went from the White House to prison."

God was indeed a God of surprises.

That evening, Tom and Gloria Pratt from Prison Fellowship hosted a small dinner party for the Colsons in a private room of the English House restaurant. Chuck gave Tom Pratt, the Chief Executive Officer of Prison Fellowship, the check from the Templeton Prize.

"It is a great privilege to give this prize money to Prison Fellowship," Chuck said. "It's because of the diligent work of the staff and volunteers around the world that I could even be considered for such an award."

The next day, as another part of the ceremonies for the Templeton Prize, Chuck addressed the British Parliament in the House of

Commons. To stand before that group would hold special historical meaning for Chuck. One of his personal heroes, a man who lived during the 1800s, had also spoken before Parliament—William Wilberforce, who, for more than fifty years, had worked to abolish slavery and to encourage a moral way of life. Through his attempts to change the prison systems and encourage moral and upright actions from people, Chuck had worked toward the same goals.

Chuck addressed another distinguished group of men and women in England. Some of the leading thinkers in England gathered for the meetings of the Tory Philosophical Society. Paul Johnson, a well-known historian, had invited Chuck to address the group.

The Philosophical Society meetings were held in the home of a member of the British Parliament, not far from the Parliament building. At one time this house had been owned by the former prime minister of England, Winston Churchill. It was a huge place—actually two homes that had been connected. On the night of the meeting, Chuck walked into an immense room with a huge fireplace. Walls of books surrounded the room, and over a hundred people gathered in several different seating areas.

Chuck and his staff had prepared for that

meeting as if they were preparing for a presidential debate. The society had proposed the topic, "Can You Be Good Without God?" Chuck thought it was an appropriate topic, and that night, in a forty-minute lecture, Chuck discussed the issues of right and wrong for a society that decided to leave God out of it. A ninety-minute question and answer session followed the talk. Many of the members of the society were not believers in Jesus Christ, but they were interested in religion. Why? Because standards of right and wrong are necessary to establish order and justice in society.

Once again, Chuck realized, his simple obedience to Jesus Christ in trying to find ways to communicate the Gospel to prisoners had opened doors for him to present that same simple message to the great, the powerful, and the wise.

* * *

The most visible public event related to the Templeton Prize was held in Chicago, Illinois, in September 1993 during the Parliament of World Religions. People from all religions came to hear the Chuck Colson's Templeton Address.

The ceremony was held in an old Gothic-type cathedral called the Rockefeller Chapel on the campus of the University of Chicago. The fourteen hundred seats were full. The ceremony had been designed by the Templeton Foundation. A Muslim leader said the opening prayer in Arabic. Then two other speakers explained the background of the Templeton Prize.

As the final speech was given, Chuck looked over his notes. Then he walked up to the platform and, for the next thirty minutes, gave a clear description of his relationship with God to an audience filled with representatives of every major religion. "The God of Abraham, Isaac, and Jacob reigns," he said. "His plan and purpose rob the future of its fears."

* * *

Later in the year, Chuck and a small group from Prison Fellowship took a whirlwind trip overseas. In ten days, they traveled around the globe to India, Singapore, Indonesia, Taiwan, Hong Kong, and Macao. In each country, they met with top government officials and visited prisons.

One of their first stops was a prison outside New Delhi, India's capital. There they met Karen Bedi, the inspector general of the New Delhi prison system. This Sikh Hindu woman had just taken over the job about five months before.

Because she believed that criminals in jail needed contact with society so that they didn't lose touch, she was very open to requests from outsiders to visit the prisons.

"Can someone take us through the prisons?" Chuck asked her.

"Oh, yes—I will," she said.

They went to a prison outside of the city. The concrete prison walls were stark but clean. Along with Congressman Bob McEwen from Ohio, who had come along to meet with officials about the justice system, Chuck jumped out of their car and headed into the prison. Karen Bedi would be interpreting for the men as they talked with the prisoners.

Chuck had heard about the innovative programs in this particular prison—classes for literacy, for example, and a program to allow the prisoners some interaction with the outside world to help with their rehabilitation.

The prison impressed Chuck. It was very clean, for one thing. And the prisoners weren't wearing uniforms but were dressed in their regular clothes. The men were locked in simple cells—very clean but furnished with only a straw mat on the floor for sleeping.

Chuck wanted to present the Gospel of Jesus Christ to the men in this prison, but he wondered: *Will this Hindu woman be willing to translate accurately for us when we talk about Christ?*

"I'm going to give you a tour of the prison," Ms. Bedi explained. "This is just a normal day, and we are having classes. Let's visit a few of them."

The courtyard they walked into was surrounded with individual cells for the prisoners. Under one shade tree, a teacher was teaching a group of the inmates to read. In another area of the courtyard, someone was teaching English. As he spoke with the men, Chuck realized that these literacy classes provided a large boost to the prisoners' morale.

A small group of about one hundred-fifty prisoners gathered to hear these visitors from the United States. Ms. Bedi introduced Chuck as the winner of the Templeton Prize. Congressman McEwen spoke first: "We're only here for one reason: because Jesus Christ has come into our lives. He has forgiven every wrong thing that we have done, and for that reason he is the most important thing in our lives." Speaking as plainly as he could, Congressman McEwen shared the Gospel of Christ—and Ms. Bedi translated his speech enthusiastically.

As he listened to the congressman's speech

Chuck Colson

winding down, Chuck reflected on the events of the past few months. Meeting with government officials around the globe, receiving a prize worth a million dollars, visiting Buckingham Palace to meet Prince Philip—and also spending time in some of the least pleasant, most out-of-the-way places on earth to meet with forgotten men: prisoners. *I don't have to think up a new message for each of those vastly different audiences,* Chuck thought, *because I only have one message worth sharing: God's power can change lives. It changed mine.*

When the congressman turned the platform over to him, Chuck stepped to the front of the group and began his speech in the same way he began each talk in the prisons: "Hello, fellow sinners. . ."